I0128321

Challenges Facing Suburban Schools

Challenges Facing Suburban Schools

Promising Responses to Changing Student Populations

Edited by Shelley B. Wepner
and Diane W. Gomez

ROWMAN & LITTLEFIELD
Lanham • Boulder • New York • London

Published by Rowman & Littlefield
A wholly owned subsidiary of The Rowman & Littlefield Publishing Group, Inc.
4501 Forbes Boulevard, Suite 200, Lanham, Maryland 20706
www.rowman.com

Unit A, Whitacre Mews, 26-34 Stannary Street, London SE11 4AB

Copyright © 2017 by Shelley B. Wepner and Diane W. Gomez

All rights reserved. No part of this book may be reproduced in any form or by any
electronic or mechanical means, including information storage and retrieval systems,
without written permission from the publisher, except by a reviewer who may quote
passages in a review.

British Library Cataloguing in Publication Information Available

Library of Congress Cataloging-in-Publication Data

978-1-4758-3282-2 (cloth : alk. paper)
978-1-4758-3283-9 (pbk. : alk. paper)
978-1-4758-3284-6 (electronic)

♾ ™ The paper used in this publication meets the minimum requirements of American
National Standard for Information Sciences Permanence of Paper for Printed Library
Materials, ANSI/NISO Z39.48-1992.

Printed in the United States of America

"Those who cannot change their minds cannot change anything."
—George Bernard Shaw

From Shelley:
To my husband Roy; and daughters, sons-in-law, and grandchildren—
Meredith, Judd, Eliza, and Sydney Grossman; Leslie, Marc, Teddy, and
Sloane Regenbaum—whose enchanting ways and courageous acts have
brought me to new heights in thinking, feeling, and believing in possibil-
ities.

From Dee:
To my husband, David; daughters; Cris, Julia, and Tori; sons-in-law Ivan
and Steven; and grandson, David Stanley who inspire me daily and open
my eyes to the powerfulness of the human spirit.

Contents

Foreword

Historians tell us that the growth of American suburbs began in the nineteenth century with the development of the railroads, which facilitated commuting. But it was the expansion of suburbs after World War II that led to the modern conception of suburbia that most of us possess—leafy neighborhoods populated by middle-class, White, English-speaking families, with a mother, father, and 2.4 children; high-quality schools; plentiful churches and shopping malls; and people flitting from place to place in their automobiles.

That rosy-eyed conception certainly wasn't always the actuality in the communities that ring our urban centers, but it was true often enough that the stereotype is not an unreasonable one. Think of the characteristically upbeat vision of suburbia promoted in *Leave It to Beaver*, *Ozzie and Harriet*, and in scads of other TV shows and movies. The worst thing that ever happened in the suburban schools in those television neighborhoods was that some child might not get into the school's talent show.

In the 1950s, American suburbs expanded dramatically, increasing their populations by 47 percent, at a time when the overall American population only grew about 19 percent. Why the big increase? One can characterize these shifts positively or negatively, and I think it is obvious that there was an admixture of both. For example, Americans had just lived through years of grinding economic depression and a harrowing world war—both of which served to put the American dream beyond reach. The economy expanded rapidly in the 1950s and 1960s—average incomes nearly tripled—and this coupled with pent-up consumer demands, federal housing efforts aimed at meeting the needs of returning soldiers, and burgeoning families (the so-called "Baby Boom") sent Americans sprawling beyond city limits. There's nothing wrong with any of that.

But on a sourer note, it is fair to point out that Americans were not just migrating toward the idylls of suburban life; they were also fleeing the new realities of our cities. The diaspora of African Americans from the South to the cities was in full swing, and as Blacks moved in, Whites moved out—their segregation guaranteed by redlining, racial steering, and discriminatory contracts. Since Blacks were generally paid less than Whites—due to differences in skills attainment, seniority, and out-and-out racism—this meant that city tax bases were shrinking. Fewer tax dollars meant less money for schools, and since urban schools were older and more costly to maintain, this led to a vicious circle, with suburban migration leading to the decline of urban schools, which, in turn, led even more families to bolt to the suburbs in pursuit of better educational opportunities for their kids. No wonder some saw the suburban ring around the cities as a "white noose."

Let's face it: Suburban schools were the "good ones," but *good* in this case did not necessarily mean the suburban schools provided greater "value added." Nevertheless, suburban schools had the best facilities and served the easiest-to-educate children (those growing up with economic advantages, whose parents were educated, whose families were intact, whose families already spoke English). Suburban schools also tended to be smaller and located in relatively low-crime areas—in the kinds of neighborhoods that teachers themselves wanted to live—and suburban districts were not typically under financial duress—all factors that helped districts to attract the choicest teachers. As immigration skyrocketed in the 1970s, the points of entry tended to be in the big cities, not the suburbs. No wonder reading test scores usually reveal yawning gaps between cities and suburbs.

So if the suburbs are so educationally privileged and fortunate, why a book on suburban education?

The simple answer is that America is on the move again. In the twenty-first century our suburbs look more like small cities than the semirural communities of *The Brady Bunch*. Population densities are on the rise. And suburban populations are becoming increasingly diverse—racially, linguistically, economically, and in terms of the composition of families.

What all that means is that suburban schools can no longer "succeed" just by doing better than schools with less-advantaged populations, since they now often serve those same students themselves. Suburban teachers now need to know how to teach children who are growing up in poverty. They need to know how to teach those who come to school without English. They need to know how to meet the needs of children whose lives may be very different than their own.

To successfully teach in the new suburbia, teachers will have to know a lot more and be aware of factors that, even recently, may have seemed irrelevant. "Children raised in poverty rarely choose to behave differently, but they are faced daily with overwhelming challenges that affluent children never have to confront, and their brains have adapted to suboptimal conditions in ways that undermine good school performance" (Jensen, 2009, p. 14). Generally, economically disadvantaged kids lack a lot of the home supports that suburban teachers have so long relied on. Instead of coming to school feeling emotionally and socially secure, poverty kids are more likely to withdraw or to act out. These kids get sick more often, too, so absences can be a big problem. And who reads to them or helps with homework? Furthermore, racial, ethnic, and linguistic diversity pose their own challenges—challenges many suburban teachers have never needed to face in the past, but that now are ubiquitous with more than 40 percent of minority children living in the suburbs.

The point isn't that such kids can't be taught effectively—they most certainly can be—but to do so suburban teachers and administrators must now develop new sensitivities, new insights, and new skills. What it took to teach well in the suburbs of old is no longer sufficient. The communities we live in have changed, and those changes have implications for what educators need to know. *Challenges Facing Suburban Schools: Promising Responses to Changing Student Populations* should provide suburban teachers and administrators a valuable leg up on developing the necessary awareness and insight to succeed under these new circumstances.

Timothy Shanahan
Distinguished Professor Emeritus
University of Illinois at Chicago

REFERENCE

Jensen, E. (2009). *Teaching with poverty in mind.* Alexandria, VA: ASCD.

Acknowledgments

It only takes one! We know from experience that, when searching for something or someone important such as a job, a partner, or a place to live, it only takes one match to fulfill a dream. When we decided to coedit this book, we knew that we would be challenging ourselves to find an editor who would understand that, while not yet universally appreciated, the concept of changing suburban schools had to be explored.

Since 2004, we have witnessed changes to our local suburban schools, listened to renowned educators' portrayal of the growing challenges associated with increased diversity in changing suburban schools, and steeped ourselves in the lives of teachers and administrators who are struggling with what had become their new reality. Yet, and unfortunately, those not living with the academic, linguistic, economic, and political pressures in and around changing suburban schools see it as nothing more than a news flash.

Tom Koerner, vice president and publisher of the education division for Rowman & Littlefield Publishing Group, was the *one* who saw the potential of bringing to the fore our idea of assembling a group of esteemed colleagues to discuss their understandings, experiences, and recommendations for a changing student population in suburban schools. We are forever appreciative that Tom recognized that this topic had a place in Rowman & Littlefield's library of professional books.

We genuinely appreciate the encouragement and guidance from associate editor Carlie Wall at Rowman & Littlefield, who first brought our idea to Tom and then coordinated the necessary details to move forward with this book. We also express thanks to Caitlin Bean at Rowman & Littlefield who helped with the book's production.

We sincerely thank a team of individuals at Manhattanville College for creating and sustaining the Changing Suburbs Institute® (CSI), the signature community outreach program of the School of Education. We especially acknowledge an anonymous donor who instigated the pursuit of CSI. She realized that her once-toney town of upper-middle-class Whites was changing to a multicultural town of low-income Hispanics.

She urged us to think differently about how we were preparing our teacher candidates for the neighboring K–12 schools because she believed that our students would not be able to address the achievement gap that was growing in her own school district and other similarly changing suburban districts. This donor helped us to conceive of the concept of CSI, which was then wholeheartedly supported and shaped by Manhattanville College's central administration and other key stakeholders.

It was the keynote speakers at our annual CSI conference and other notable researchers focused on the changing suburbs that prompted us to coedit this book because their discoveries, experiences, and recommendations would resonate with those mindful of demographic shifts and accompanying educational challenges in suburban schools. We acknowledge with enormous admiration and immeasurable appreciation our chapter authors for their important contributions to this book. Their professionalism and responsiveness were beyond expectation.

We also thank graduate assistant Sung Kim for his diligent and capable assistance in identifying research to support our work. Finally, we thank our spouses for their steadfast love and support as we pursued this project. Shelley's spouse, Roy, learned to live with a wife who created makeshift offices—replete with a laptop, papers, and food—wherever and whenever they traveled so that she could take advantage of her "free" time to work on this book. His unconditional love and brilliant guidance have enabled Shelley to persist during the most trying moments. Dee's husband, David, pitched in to do whatever was necessary to keep the home front harmonious while Dee strove to meet deadlines. His constant, loving encouragement kept her going throughout the writing and editing process.

Introduction

There is a phenomenon in education that needs our attention. This phenomenon is happening in suburban schools across the United States because of a changing student population that is racially, culturally, ethnically, linguistically, and economically different from mainstream, monolingual, middle-class, White students. This changing student population poses a new set of educational, administrative, social, and political challenges to suburban schools.

Teachers and administrators are perplexed and dismayed by the ever-widening achievement gap that highlights differences between the privileged and less privileged. These educators are living with a new kind of risk because their previously successful instructional policies and practices simply are not working. They are frustrated because their changing suburban schools are not included in the same prominent pieces of funding legislation as their most urban counterparts.

Yet, unbeknownst to too many others, these teachers and administrators are working in schools that now have deep pockets of poverty, undocumented immigrants, linguistic challenges, and achievement issues that must be addressed in order to provide their students with rich life experiences and optimistic futures.

PURPOSE OF *CHALLENGES FACING SUBURBAN SCHOOLS: PROMISING RESPONSES TO CHANGING STUDENT POPULATIONS*

Challenges Facing Suburban Schools: Promising Responses to Changing Student Populations addresses this new phenomenon with a comprehensive and in-depth overview of the concept of changing suburban schools. This coedited book describes the impact that an increasingly diverse student population has on twenty-first-century suburban schools. It also presents what can and should be done to help K–12 school district administrators and teachers address this growing phenomenon across the nation. This eight-chapter book:

- provides a demographic, political, economic, and sociological overview of the changing nature of suburban schools;
- describes the nature of student diversity in the changing suburbs and issues with student achievement;
- identifies administrative responsibilities and program structures for working with a changing student population;
- proposes ways to reduce the achievement gap, most notably in literacy;
- looks at how to use "whole child" assessment protocols to provide support for such students; and
- delves into parent inequities within changing suburban districts and offers ideas for closing the parent gap.

Challenges Facing Suburban Schools: Promising Responses to Changing Student Populations is written for those affiliated with education who have responsibility for teaching about, proposing, legislating, and implementing policies related to instruction and assessment at the national, state, and school district levels. It serves as a source of professional development in acknowledging and understanding reasons for and challenges with demographic shifts in school districts so that teachers and administrators can begin to develop programs and pathways for student success and parent engagement.

This book serves as a repository of information for legislators, policymakers, and educational researchers for developing new schema about a segment of the student and parent population that now is living in suburban areas without traditional roots as advantaged suburbanites or disadvantaged urbanites.

RATIONALE FOR *CHALLENGES FACING SUBURBAN SCHOOLS: PROMISING RESPONSES TO CHANGING STUDENT POPULATIONS*

The demography of public school enrollment in the suburbs continues to change quite dramatically, "with students of color comprising an increasing proportion of the whole" (Frankenberg & Kotok, 2013, p. 112). Many of these students come from families of lower socioeconomic status (SES) and live in homes where languages other than English are spoken. Suburban schools are experiencing multiple challenges in providing the appropriate educational opportunities for all students as a result of governmental rulings, economic restraints, and community perspectives and interferences.

Community cultures are colliding, parents are living with economic and social gaps, and educators are daunted by the challenges. As a result, suburban students are experiencing chronic achievement gaps, with students of color achieving well below their White counterparts. The magnitude of this changing suburban phenomenon continues to be below the radar screen of national policymakers and the media.

Any crisis in American schools focuses on urban schools, and not suburban schools. Yet the same student achievement challenges occurring in urban schools are ever present in suburban schools, making the changing suburban school phenomenon a necessary focal point for policymakers, legislators, entrepreneurs, community leaders, and educators if *all* students are to succeed in this century.

Today's suburban educators are trying to come to grips with a changing student population by adapting and adjusting instruction in relation to high-stakes testing and data-driven instruction around a common core of standards. They also are trying to identify ways to satisfy a diverse parent population. This is no small task. A classic case of the changing suburban school phenomenon arises when a district's catchment area continues to service the same number of students from wealthy towns and neighborhoods with an increasing number of students from much less wealthy parts of the same district.

Vast differences exist in the neighborhood schools at the elementary level between the very affluent residents who are on one side of the district's catchment area and the often-impoverished residents who are on the other side of the same district's catchment area. Although the students from these two sides of town do not necessarily interact during the elementary school years, they are thrust together during the middle school and high school years. The elementary schools have very different needs in relation to instructional assistance to address the same districtwide curriculum.

Parents of the affluent children are not necessarily interested in using their tax dollars to supplement the schools that need additional funds to provide personnel, programs, and materials to help those students who have not had the economic, experiential, and linguistic advantages at home to prepare for the demands of a core curriculum. These parents typically have the time and resources to make their wishes known. On the other hand, parents of the less affluent children do not have the same leverage with the schools to access the resources for their children's achievement needs.

Tensions arise when district administrators and teachers have to account for achievement differences and put into place plans for closing an achievement gap. These plans invariably involve new programs, additional personnel, and structural reconfigurations that are not supported by local taxpayers.

District administrators are caught in the middle of trying to satisfy their affluent and high-achieving families who help the district's overall "report card" rating and provide the necessary instructional support for their less privileged students.

If these district administrators accede to their more affluent community members, they are inadvertently harming a growing pool of students in need of help and perpetuating their district's achievement gap. If these district administrators take a stand against their affluent and vocal community members to use district funds to provide needed support structures for students in need, they run the risk of "white flight" from their districts and, worse yet, put their own jobs in jeopardy because of political ramifications with their own school boards.

Challenges Facing Suburban Schools: Promising Responses to Changing Student Populations was written to bring to the fore these real-life issues that are jeopardizing teachers' and administrators' ability to serve all students appropriately. In addition to proposing suggestions for addressing some of these challenges, this book also attempts to enlighten those in the position to influence policies for this growing phenomenon across America.

BACKDROP TO *CHALLENGES FACING SUBURBAN SCHOOLS: PROMISING RESPONSES TO CHANGING STUDENT POPULATIONS*

The basis for this book comes from the authors' firsthand experiences with changing suburban schools, work with school district administrators and teachers on their efforts to accommodate a changing student population, and conversations with other prominent educators across the nation with similar experiences in pursuit of ideas, initiatives, and solutions related to an increasingly persistent achievement gap between the haves and have nots within the same school districts.

These authors have been focused through their teaching, research, and publication on specific aspects and challenges of educating an increasingly diverse student population. The authors represent different parts of the United States (Arizona, California, Louisiana, Massachusetts, Michigan, New York, Pennsylvania, and Texas), are affiliated with either a college, major university, or research center focused on English language education, and have conducted quantitative or qualitative research with and about stakeholders in the changing suburbs.

Seven of the fourteen authors have contributed as keynote speakers, coauthors, or participants with a special initiative, the Changing Suburbs Institute (CSI), dedicated to learning about and working with changing suburban schools in the New York area. CSI is a grassroots, school-university-community collaborative that was established in recognition of the increasing diversity in suburban school districts and the need to ensure that practicing and prospective teachers are prepared to teach an increasingly diverse student population.

DESCRIPTION OF *CHALLENGES FACING SUBURBAN SCHOOLS: PROMISING RESPONSES TO CHANGING STUDENT POPULATIONS*

Fourteen authors share their insights, research, theories, experiences, and recommendations about the changing suburban school phenomenon to help educators with their jobs and students with their learning. The ideas and viewpoints are intended to (1) improve current conditions at the district, school, classroom, and community levels, and (2) provide information to those who have control over critical levers for affecting how changing suburban schools are situated.

This book has three unique features:

1. Each chapter is authored or coauthored by experts who already have multiple publications related to that topic.
2. Each chapter includes three bullets at the beginning to highlight the main ideas to be presented.
3. Each chapter has three provocative questions at the end to generate discussion about the ideas presented and future endeavors.

The book begins with a demographic, political, economic, and sociological portrayal of changing suburban schools. The first two chapters serve as a springboard for the presentation of different ideas and viewpoints on challenges and solutions for helping with the growing achievement gap that exists within changing suburban districts because of racial, cultural, social, economic, and language differences.

Chapter 1, *Demography and Educational Politics in the Changing Suburbs*, written by Stephen Kotok and Erica Frankenberg, presents a demographic and political overview of the changing nature of suburban school communities and how different jurisdictional issues within municipalities affect how school districts address increasing student diversity.

Chapter 2, *Race, Ethnicity, and Social Capital in the Changing Suburbs*, written by Carl L. Bankston III and Stephen J. Caldas, reveals that parents from minority backgrounds, particularly African Americans and Hispanics, have less total social capital than Whites, even when SES is not really a factor in changing suburban school districts. The authors discuss how this social capital phenomenon leads to achievement gaps, parent outrage, parent flight, and difficulty in getting budget support from the community.

The next two chapters focus on administrators' plights in changing suburban schools and ways that school leaders can work with their teachers and communities to bring about needed changes.

Chapter 3, *Administrators' Accountabilities in Changing Suburban Schools,* written by the editors, Shelley B. Wepner and Diane W. Gómez, describes the political, fiscal, educational, and community pressures that school district and school-based administrators encounter as a result of their increasingly diverse student and parent populations. The authors use these challenges as a basis for recommending optional organizational structures, programs, and professional development opportunities that can be pursued.

Chapter 4, *Lessons for Leaders about Educating English Learners*, written by Douglas Fisher and Nancy Frey, discusses the significant role that school leaders have in ensuring that English learners (ELs) access quality learning experiences. The authors describe how school leaders can help teachers provide significant amounts of relevant instructional time to practicing language so that ELs can progress in content and language learning. They also explain how school leaders must track the progress of their ELs to ensure that the school's language assistance program is educationally sound.

The next three chapters offer ideas for helping to reduce the achievement gap through specific instructional and assessment protocols.

Chapter 5, *A Conceptual Framework for the Educational Success of Dual Language Learners: Reducing the Achievement Gap*, written by Eugene E. García, presents a conceptual framework for addressing the needs of dual language learners (DLLs). His framework emphasizes the need to focus on the family structure and culture, educational practices, community and societal circumstances, and DLLs' brain development. He explains that because DLLs often develop and learn in unique environments and ways, DLLs' educational opportunities should account for these experiences.

Chapter 6, *Effective Literacy Instruction for English Learners*, written by María Paula Ghiso, explains how literacy instruction for students who speak a language other than English need not be "either-or"—either learning the power codes of academic literacies in English or honoring students' home languages and community literacy practices. She describes specific pedagogical techniques for developing literacy that are directed toward "both-and" by drawing on community knowledge and situating learning within a broader social and political context.

Chapter 7, *Data-Driven Decisions on Effective Performance Measures of English Learners*, written by Debbie Zacarian, discusses how to collect common data of ELs to identify, create, implement, and strengthen programming. Distinctions are described between ELs who (1) possess school-matched academic language and literacy skills and (2) do not yet possess these skills so that data-driven practices for ELs are strengthened.

The last of the eight chapters focuses on parents of the changing student population, with specific ideas on how to engage them in the schools.

Chapter 8, *Closing the Parent Gap in Changing School Districts*, written by Patricia A. Edwards, Lisa Domke, and Kristen White, presents ideas for administrators and teachers to use to reconceptualize and reach out to a changing suburban school's parent population. The strategies focus on differentiated parenting and parentally appropriate activities that promote communication and connections with parents from diverse cultures.

Although written with different voices, the chapters communicate a shared perspective of recognizing the unique features of a changing suburban school and finding ways to assist with this new demographic reality. We hope that the information and ideas presented encourage you to design your own blueprint for action.

REFERENCE

Frankenberg, E., & Kotok, S. (2013). Demography and educational politics in the suburban marketplace. *Peabody Journal of Education, 88*(1), 112–126.

Chapter One

Demography and Educational Politics in the Changing Suburbs

Stephen Kotok and Erica Frankenberg

- Overall, the population of students attending suburban public schools is increasingly diverse racially, economically, and linguistically.
- Suburban diversity is not evenly distributed, with some districts and metropolitan areas being much more segregated by race and poverty.
- Increasing diversity provides an opportunity for suburban school districts to create more integrated student bodies and teacher corps as well as multicultural and bilingual curriculums, though the implementation of these goals is politically challenging for districts not accustomed to their changing demographics.

The American suburbs of the twenty-first century look vastly different in economics and demography from those of the mid-twentieth century, when suburban expansion first exploded. Following World War II, lily-white suburbs sprouted up around many of America's largest cities, spurred by advances in transportation (Monkkonen, 1980) as well as specific programs such as the 1948 Housing Bill aimed at working-class Whites (Fischer, 2008).

This exodus to the suburbs continued throughout the 1960s and 1970s, and racial segregation usually spread concurrently as a result of individual preferences as well as governmental policies that hindered racially integrated suburbs (Rothstein, 2015). Yet, in spite of the social and political conditions of the latter twentieth century, racially diverse suburbs emerged in American metropolitan areas to varying degrees (Frey, 2011). This chapter examines increasing racial, economic, and linguistic diversity in the context of suburban public schools.

As the United States transitions to being a majority minority country, it is important to understand the demographic trends in suburban school districts and the political landscape that accompanies such a shift. Current demographics of the suburban public school population are presented utilizing data from the U.S. Census and the Common Core of Data universe. Secondly, this chapter contains a discussion of key political issues—opportunities as well as challenges—currently facing many suburban school districts.

Moreover, it explores how such issues differ depending on the local context. Given that most students in major metropolitan areas attend schools in the suburbs instead of central cities, understanding the demographic complexity of suburbia is critical for educators in the twenty-first century.

A CHANGING DEMOGRAPHY

The suburban landscape looks very different today than it did just a few decades ago. A report from the Brookings Institute (Frey, 2011) used census data to illuminate many of the major demographic shifts in American metropolitan areas over the last three decades. Some of the key findings include:

- The share of minority residents living in the suburbs almost doubled between 1990 and 2010 from 19 percent to 35 percent.
- The population of Latinos living in suburban communities increased by over 8 million people between 2000 and 2010, adding to previous decades of increasing Latino population.
- Of the one hundred largest metropolitan areas, sixteen of them now have suburbs that, when combined (e.g., the entire group of suburbs in that metro area), are majority minority, an increase from only four in 1990.

These increasingly diverse suburbs look vastly different depending on the region of the country. For instance, the many majority minority suburbs of California are dominated by Latinos and, in the case of the Bay Area, Latinos and Asians. Washington, DC, is the only majority minority suburban area where African Americans are the largest minority, though there are several other diverse southern metropolitan areas such as Atlanta, Richmond, and Memphis that have extremely large shares of African American residents.

Compared to other community types—rural, town, and urban—overall, suburban schools enroll the most students and draw the most diverse range of student demographics. Although almost half of the school districts in the United States are located in rural areas, nearly 43 percent of all public school students attend a suburban school.

Whereas the demographics of urban public schools differ greatly from the city itself due to high levels of private school enrollment, the demographics of American public schools in suburbia more closely reflect the community in terms of diversity (Reardon & Yun, 2002). Therefore, it is useful to analyze the school-level demographics in addition to those residential demographics provided by the census.

Table 1.1 provides data on the number of districts and proportions of each race/ethnicity by community for the 2013–2014 school year. The suburban enrollment is still majority White, but almost 40 percent of the students attending suburban schools are a race or ethnicity other than White. Although the greater shares of Black and Latino students attend urban schools, over 20 percent of suburban students are Black, and almost 17 percent of suburban students were Latino.

Moreover, Asians made up around 5 percent of all suburban students, their highest share of all four community types. Further, increasingly large shares of Black and Latino students have suburbanized (not shown in the table): 38 percent of *all* Black students went to suburban schools compared to 47 percent in urban schools. For Latinos, 40 percent of *all* students attended a suburban school compared to 45 percent enrolled in urban schools.

Despite the increasing share of suburban enrollment among minority students, Black and Latino students remain extremely segregated in suburban schools. Orfield and Frankenberg (2014) examined exposure rates for suburban students living in large, medium, and small metropolitan areas and found that suburban students were segregated, though the segregation was lower than in urban areas and it varied by metro size.

For instance, the typical White student in a large metro suburban area attended a school with 70 percent Whites, while the typical Black student attended a suburban school with 29 percent White students, and the average Latino attended a school with less than 25 percent White students. Such wide

Table 1.1. Racial Composition of Public Schools by Community Type, 2013–2014

	Suburban	Urban	Town	Rural
% White	61.81	28.02	69.98	78.84
% Black	20.44	37.53	7.45	4.20
% Latino	16.83	26.60	15.78	9.68
% Asian	4.98	3.81	1.82	0.76
% Two or More Races	2.68	3.15	2.77	2.25
% American Indian	0.53	0.89	2.89	4.23
Number of Districts	3,802	2,635	2,685	7,489
Number of Students (in millions)	21.3	15.7	5.6	7.3

disparities indicate that these suburbs are incredibly segregated, often with inner-ring suburbs now being mostly minority in many cases.

Although White suburban students living in medium- and small-sized metros attended schools with even greater shares of White students (73 percent and 75 percent), Black students were typically more integrated in these smaller metro suburbs. On average, Black students at these small and medium metro suburbs enrolled in schools where almost half of the students were White. Conversely, the typical Latino student in small and medium metro suburbs only attended a school where around a third of the students were White.

In addition to racial diversity, the overall suburban landscape has shifted in terms of economic and linguistic diversity. In regards to low-income students, on average, over one-third of suburban students received a free/reduced lunch (FRL). In 2013–2014, 37 percent of suburban students received FRL compared to 45 percent in rural schools, 49 percent in town schools, and 63 percent in urban schools (according to the authors' analysis of raw data from the National Center for Education Statistics [NCES; n.d.]).

Figure 1.1 shows the breakdown of suburban schools by FRL concentration based on the percentage of students receiving FRL: 0–25 percent; 25–50 percent; 50–75 percent; and 75–100 percent.[1] The plurality of schools (40.5 percent) enrolled fewer than 25 percent FRL students, yet over 19 percent of suburban schools had between 50 percent and 75 percent FRL students, and 11 percent had over 75 percent FRL students.

Of course, some suburban districts serve far greater numbers of FRL students. For instance, suburbs in the South and West had higher poverty rates than other regions, while the suburbs in the Midwest had the most rapidly increasing levels of poverty as a consequence of industrial decline (Frankenberg, 2013). Moreover, rates of low-income students also fluctuate among suburban districts within metropolitan areas. For instance, Riverview Gardens School District, located north of St. Louis, Missouri, served 96 percent FRL students, while Clayton School District, located directly west of St. Louis, only enrolled 13 percent FRL students. Although suburban students thus are advantaged compared to their urban and rural counterparts, the fact that over one-third of suburban students are low-income, and that one in nine suburban students attends a school with between 75 percent and 100 percent of students poor or near-poor, complicates the notion that affluence lines the streets of all suburbia. It cannot be assumed that *all* suburban students have safe places to complete homework or have reliable transportation to get to school events. Moreover, attendance at high-poverty schools disadvantages students through resources, peer effects, and teacher attrition.

According to the analysis of 2013–2014 NCES data, more than 5 percent of suburban students were classified as English learners (ELs), second only to 7.9 percent of urban students classified as such. Yet, similar to poverty,

Concentration of FRL Students

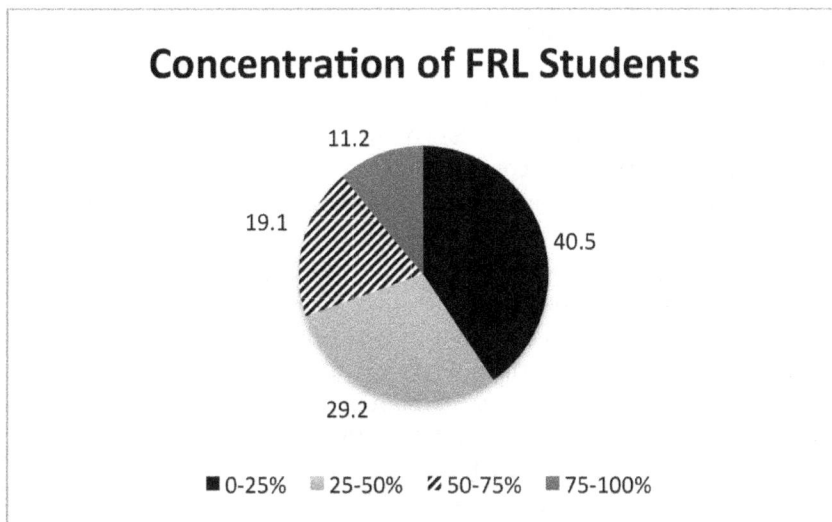

Figure 1.1.   Concentration of FRL Students

these EL students are not spread evenly, with some suburban districts having extremely high proportions of their students speaking languages other than English.

Suburban communities in border states such as Texas, New Mexico, Arizona, and California are especially diverse linguistically, but there are increasing numbers of EL students in new immigrant destinations in the Midwest and Southeast (Lichter, Parisi, Taquino, & Grice, 2010; Lowenhaupt, 2016). It is no surprise that almost half the students are EL in La Joya Independent School District, a small suburban district on the Texas–Mexico border. Conversely, it comes as quite a surprise to many that one in five students are classified as EL in Lamphere School District, a large suburban school district south of Detroit.

POLITICS OF CHANGING SCHOOL DEMOGRAPHY

Politically, the increasing diversity in suburban schools presents both challenges and opportunities for school districts. Whereas some districts have a longer history with rich diversity, other districts are experiencing these changes for the first time, meaning their teachers may be less prepared, they may find themselves dealing with resistance from parents to more inclusive curricular changes, or they simply lack highly qualified bilingual teachers needed for EL students.

Legal and Political Landscape

The postwar expansion of suburbia led to an intense fragmentation of school governance in metropolitan areas (Bischoff, 2008; Frankenberg & Kotok, 2013). Theoretically, families could shop for a school district based on local preferences for curriculum, facilities, or some other amenity. However, in reality, there were multiple economic and social factors preventing families, especially those of color, from having equal access to homes in many suburban communities.

Often, White families with the financial means to move sought out predominantly White suburban communities (Charles, 2005). Even when middle-class Black families attempt to move to these wealthier mostly White suburbs, they are often confronted with various types of housing discrimination, including steering by realtors to high minority suburbs or urban areas (Massey & Mullan, 1984; Shapiro, 2005; Turner & Ross, 2005).

Given such inequality, many civil rights activists sought a metropolitan solution for K–12 schools based on shared educational goals between suburbs and the city. Yet, the U.S. Supreme Court effectively ended this movement when they ruled against the plaintiffs in *Milliken v. Bradley* (1974). In *Milliken*, the plaintiffs wanted to implement cross-district bussing in Detroit since the city and its various suburbs were already unified through the local economy and other public goods such as roads and utilities (Garnett, 2007; Logan, Oakley, & Stowell, 2008).

By rejecting the metropolitan solution, it discouraged regional cooperation between suburbs and created a fragmented system where homebuyers could easily avoid racially integrated schools if they possessed financial means, as there are currently hundreds of suburban districts operating around America's largest cities and in close proximity to one another but with distinct racial and economic enrollments. Any cooperation between districts in terms of shared resources or inter-district transfers occurs primarily on a voluntary basis. The inter-district desegregation programs that exist are incredibly popular among families, yet they remain few and operate with limited funding.

Suburban Economics

Overall, suburbia is relatively advantaged financially, but pockets of poverty also pervade suburban America, especially some of the older inner-ring suburbs (Frankenberg, 2013). As noted previously, over one-third of students in suburbs receive FRL, with some districts having extremely high concentrations of poverty.

Politically, suburban poverty is often not as widely covered by the media as urban poverty, and suburbs may also lack many of the safety nets or public programs that exist to help the urban poor. Predominantly non-White suburban schools have been found to be even more financially disadvantaged than their urban counterparts, considering they have a tax base that is 30 percent lower than central cities despite an almost identical median income in both communities (Orfield & Luce, 2012).

Many structural challenges affect these lower-income, more diverse suburban communities and districts. Sub-prime lenders disproportionally targeted minorities, many of whom purchased homes in suburban communities (Bocian, Li, & Ernst, 2008; Rothstein, 2015). A spatial mismatch often occurs in these poorer suburban communities, where very few jobs exist in the immediate area and the communities lack the public transportation infrastructure common in most American central cities, thus limiting the job options for lower-income and lower-skill residents.

Moreover, whereas cities reap some benefits in terms of taxes on industry, these struggling suburban districts often lack this valuable tax resource. Finally, the dense population of cities often translates to a density of social services, but such services are often lacking in suburbia, where fragments of suburban poverty spread throughout a metropolitan area. These various challenges make suburban districts with higher concentrations of low-income households especially vulnerable to the Great Recession.

IMPLICATIONS OF CHANGING DEMOGRAPHY WITHIN SCHOOLS

In addition to the already-discussed macro-level implications of suburban diversity, there are also many policy implications for individual schools. As schools become more diverse, they must think critically about their procedures and curriculums to ensure equal access as well as social justice in terms of discipline. Some key areas for consideration include: (1) tracking and ability grouping; (2) disparate discipline; (3) bilingual resources; and (4) inclusive curriculums.

Tracking and Ability Grouping

Ability grouping refers to the practice of placing elementary (and sometimes older) students into groups based on perceived academic ability, while *tracking* refers to the practice of enrolling secondary students into courses based on perceived academic ability. Several studies document that even when Black and Latino students attend more affluent schools, they are placed in lower-level groups or classes regardless of academic aptitude (Gándara, 2005; Oakes, 1995).

Notably, entry into these advanced courses can advantage students for postsecondary opportunities (Bromberg & Theokas, 2014). Suburban schools that use tracking and grouping need to be aware of these tendencies toward racial bias and either work to ensure equity or experiment with detracking, placing everybody in the same challenging courses regardless of perceived ability (Burris & Welner, 2007).

Disparate Discipline

Another aspect of schools pertains to the disparate discipline of Black and Latino students, especially males (Monroe, 2009). The disparate discipline measures have been documented from preschool through high school. Lewis and Diamond (2015) found such disparities existed even in a very affluent, racially integrated suburban school in the Midwest. Such unequal treatment of students hinders academic opportunity, alienates minority students, and further strains race relations in these communities.

Given the implicit racial biases among many suburban teachers and administrators, Lewis and Diamond (2015) ultimately recommend schools pursue alternative discipline strategies such as restorative justice, a system where students seek to repair any damage to the school community rather than simply receive exclusionary punishment such as suspension or expulsion.

Lack of Diversity in Teachers and Administrators

An often-overlooked aspect of school integration efforts, which was a provision of most court-ordered desegregation plans, is that that teachers needed to be integrated as well. Diverse teachers benefit students in many ways (Cohen, 1980; Villegas & Lucas, 2002). Students of color especially benefit from having teachers of color who can serve as professional role models. They can strengthen relationships between the family, school, and community, and ensure the school is inviting to students of all cultures. At the same time, White students also greatly benefit from a diverse faculty, especially since they are often the most isolated racial group.

Despite these clear advantages of having a diverse faculty, suburban teachers, like suburban students, are often segregated. Frankenberg (2013) found that overall, the racial composition of suburban teachers closely reflects the national teacher corps in general with about 85 percent of teachers being White, 5 percent Latino, 7 percent Black, 3 percent Asian, and 0.03 percent American Indian.

Such numbers already illuminate an underrepresentation of minority teachers, but these teachers are additionally segregated in their schools. For instance, the average suburban White teacher only works with 10 percent of teachers who are not White. Moreover, these mostly White teachers are not representative of their student bodies on average. In Bristol's (2014) work on supporting teachers of color, he urged districts to not only recruit teachers of color but also ensure they are retained once they are hired.

Addressing the Needs of ELs

As mentioned, Latinos and to a lesser extent Asians make up some of the largest increases in suburban school enrollments. Among these groups, a significant share of students are also immigrants who speak a language other than English. An influx of immigrant students adds great cultural diversity to the school setting, but also potentially poses a challenge for districts ill-equipped in terms of bilingual teachers, professional development, and other important resources (Lowenhaupt, 2016).

Many of these new immigrant destinations, communities without a long history of immigrants, address the EL needs by simply adding on an English language immersion class or having EL students pulled out of class occasionally for assistance (Hopkins, Lowenhaupt, & Sweet, 2015). However, Hopkins and her colleagues (2015) caution against this piecemeal approach and instead encourage district leaders to make sure *all* staff members are trained in serving EL students.

Curricular Choices

As the United States becomes more diverse, the need for a more inclusive curriculum gains importance. For too long, district curriculums took a very Eurocentric approach to the arts and humanities. Although it behooves all districts to integrate multicultural content, it is especially important in the most racially and ethnically diverse districts (Banks, 1993). Moreover, depending on the racial/ethnic composition of the student body, the district may choose to illuminate certain cultures as well.

For instance, districts in Arizona and Texas have sought to add ethnic studies classes to highlight Latino literature and history. Notably, the addition of ethnic studies classes has been found to improve several academic outcomes of minority students (Dee & Penner, 2016) and provide a new perspective for the students whose culture is not the focus of the course. Suburban districts may meet resistance from residents who feel that a more inclusive curriculum "waters down" the so-called important concepts (Vasquez Heilig, Brown, & Brown, 2012). Therefore, suburban districts must promote multiculturalism by providing evidence on its benefits to all students.

OPPORTUNITIES OF THE NEW SUBURBAN DIVERSITY

Despite the various challenges for suburban schools experiencing shifts in demography, diversity in suburban school districts foremost provides a great opportunity to re-envision public schooling in a way urban public schools have often failed. Specifically, districts are able to pursue the goal of racially and socioeconomically diverse schools. This goal is notable, since such diversity has been shown to provide extensive academic and social benefit for both White and minority students (Mickelson & Nkomo, 2012).

Whereas racial integration of schools in a large school district such as Philadelphia or Baltimore is nearly impossible without incorporating surrounding districts given the long history of housing and school segregation, the demographics of suburban areas outside such central cities may lend themselves to more diverse districts. While Whites make up less than 10 percent of the public school students in some of the most hypersegregated cities, the sheer number of Whites living in suburban areas alongside students of color makes a goal such as racially integrated schools a much more feasible possibility in suburbia.

There are many different roadmaps for achieving racially and economically diverse suburban communities, and the successful implementation of the plans depends on the local political context. Since many school districts in the South are countywide, it theoretically makes metropolitan options involving suburbs and central cities more feasible from a legal standpoint.

Some counties such as Hillsborough County, Florida, effectively used magnets for many years in order to establish several racially integrated schools. Unfortunately, in recent years, Hillsborough schools have become more segregated as the courts lifted their supervision and as school enrollments became more tightly coupled with racially segregated neighborhood boundaries. Other county districts such as Wake County, North Carolina (metropolitan Raleigh), had a plan that economically integrated the schools, including those from suburbia, but it ultimately was abandoned following what some saw as an "outside" takeover of the school board (Ciolli, 2011).

Both the Hillsborough and Wake County cases demonstrate the difficulty in maintaining a committed coalition to ensure integrated schools. Conversely, examples of suburban districts that have maintained racially and economically integrated schools using a mixture of magnet schools and a managed choice student assignment policy include Berkeley, California, and Jefferson County, Kentucky (a city-county district including Louisville).

Most integration plans rely on municipalities voluntarily participating either through multi-municipal school districts or through inter-district choice plans allowing students to transfer between districts. Yet these plans tend to be most effective at integrating students only when they have explicit goals and plans such as in the case of Wake County. Race- and income-neutral plans often further stratify students by income and race, as higher socioeconomic parents have more access to choice or use their political capital to zone schools in a way that maintains social boundaries (Cobb & Glass, 2009; Holme, Carkhum, & Rangel, 2013).

Although suburban districts benefit academically and socially by implementing diversity initiatives, it requires an extensive commitment from the community, the school board, and the administration. Federal funds and expertise are available to help suburban districts that are interested in reducing racially isolated schools or creating more diversity.

When it comes to politics of language, many districts, including some of the most affluent ones, are starting to understand the various cognitive and social benefits afforded by a dual-language program. In fact, studies indicate that children attending dual-language programs starting in kindergarten outperform their peers academically starting in middle school and continuing into higher education and beyond (Thomas & Collier, 1998). A survey of Colorado parents found that many English- and Spanish-speaking parents sought dual language schools (Shannon & Milian, 2002).

Increasingly, English-speaking parents recognize the academic and human capital benefits for their children, while non-English speakers benefit from a strong curriculum taught partially in their native language. In fact, as of 2010, at least 368 such programs existed across the country, a number that has increased rapidly since the 1990s (Gándara, 2011). Thus, it behooves suburban communities to embrace dual-language programs and schools in order to attract highly involved parents and as a constructive approach to providing equal status interaction for students across racial/ethnic lines.

CONCLUSION

The suburban school landscape, similar to the country as a whole, is becoming more diverse in terms of race/ethnicity, social background, and language status. Yet the changes to suburban demographics are occurring, on average, far more rapidly than in other types of communities. Such changes in suburban demography open a door of opportunity for these districts and the students they educate.

Specifically, there is the potential for achieving racially and economically integrated suburban schools in a way that has mostly eluded urban districts over the last decades, and could benefit students and their communities. In terms of ELs, suburban districts can at least ensure all EL students receive high-quality bilingual services, but if there is political capacity, these districts can also improve their schools by offering valuable dual-language programs.

While suburban districts may not have as much experience educating these newly diverse enrollments and thus may have initial logistical and political challenges to implementing such policies, the educational and social benefits of programs to create more racially, economically, and linguistically diverse schools are likely to prove quite substantial in the long run, providing a foundation for stability and growth in the coming decades of continued demographic transformation of suburbia.

REFLECTION QUESTIONS

1. Does it make sense to talk about "suburban districts" given the vast differences between them? If so, why? If no, why not?
2. How can suburban districts proactively respond to changing demographics to be welcoming to families of all backgrounds, even when teachers and administrators may be overwhelmingly White?
3. How can districts work together across boundary lines to provide more integrated opportunities for students of color and low-income students in suburbia?

NOTE

1. In order to avoid overlap, 25–50 percent began at 25.0001 percent and ended at 50.00 percent, and so forth.

REFERENCES

Banks, J. A. (1993). Multicultural education: Historical development, dimensions, and practice. *Review of Research in Education, 19*(1), 3–49.

Bischoff, K. (2008). School district fragmentation and racial residential segregation: How do boundaries matter? *Social Science Research, 38*, 55–70.

Bocian, D. G., Li, W., & Ernst, K. S. (2008). Race, ethnicity and subprime home loan pricing. *Journal of Economics and Business, 60*(1), 110–124.

Bristol, T. (2014). *Black men of the classroom: An exploration of how the organizational conditions, characteristics, and dynamics in schools affect Black male teachers' pathways into the profession.* Unpublished doctoral dissertation, Columbia University, New York, NY.

Bromberg, M., & Theokas, C. (2014). *Falling out of the lead: Following high achievers through high school and beyond.* Washington, DC: Education Trust.

Burris, C. C., & Welner, K. G. (2007). The potential of detracking: Closing the achievement gap. In E. Frankenberg & G. Orfield (Eds.), *Lessons in integration: Realizing the promise of racial diversity in our nation's public schools* (pp. 207–227). Charlottesville, VA: University of Virginia Press.

Charles, C. Z. (2005). How racial discrimination affects the search for housing. In X. D. Briggs (Ed.), *The geography of opportunity: Race and housing in metropolitan America* (pp. 81–102). Washington, DC: Brookings Institute Press.

Ciolli, A. (2011). Economic integration of schools: Evaluating the Wake County experiment. *University of Massachusetts Law Review, 6*(1), 57–77.

Cobb, C. D., & Glass, G. V. (2009). School choice in a post-desegregation world. *Peabody Journal of Education, 84*(2), 262–278.

Cohen, E. G. (1980). Design and redesign of the desegregated school: Problems of status, power, and conflict. In W. G. Stephan & J. R. Feagin (Eds.), *School desegregation: Past, present, and future* (pp. 251–278). New York, NY: Plenum.

Dee, T., & Penner, E. (2016). *The causal effects of cultural relevance: Evidence from an ethnic studies curriculum* (National Bureau of Economic Research No. 21865). Cambridge, MA: National Bureau of Economic Research.

Fischer, M. J. (2008). Shifting geographies: Examining the role of suburbanization in Blacks' declining segregation. *Urban Affairs Review, 43*(10), 475–496.

Frankenberg, E. (2013). Wither the suburban ideal? Understanding contemporary suburban school contexts. In G. L. Sunderman (Ed.), *Charting reform, achieving equity in a diverse nation* (pp. 207–227). Charlotte, NC: Information Age Publishing.

Frankenberg, E., & Kotok, S. (2013). Demography and educational politics in the suburban marketplace. *Peabody Journal of Education, 88*(1), 112–126.

Frey, W. H. (2011). *State of metropolitan America: Race and ethnicity.* Washington, DC: Brookings Institution. Retrieved from http://brookings.edu/metro

Gándara, P. C. (2005). *Fragile futures: Risk and vulnerability among Latino high achievers.* Princeton, NJ: Policy Information Center, Educational Testing Service.

Gándara, P. C. (2011). Latinos, language, and segregation. In E. Frankenberg & E. DeBray (Eds.), *Integrating schools in a changing society: New policies and legal options for a multicultural generation* (pp. 265–277). Chapel Hill, NC: University of North Carolina Press.

Garnett, N. S. (2007). Suburbs as exit, suburbs as entrance. *Michigan Law Review, 106*(2), 277–304.

Holme, J. J., Carkhum, R., & Rangel, V. S. (2013). High pressure reform: Examining urban schools' response to multiple school choice policies. *The Urban Review, 45*(2), 167–196.

Hopkins, M., Lowenhaupt, R., & Sweet, T. M. (2015). Organizing English learner instruction in new immigrant destinations district infrastructure and subject-specific school practice. *American Educational Research Journal, 52*(3), 408–439.

Lewis, A. E., & Diamond, J. B. (2015). *Despite the best intentions: How racial inequality thrives in good schools.* New York: Oxford University Press.

Lichter, D. T., Parisi, D., Taquino, M. C., & Grice, S. M. (2010). Residential segregation in new Latino destinations: Cities, suburbs, and rural communities compared. *Social Science Research, 39*(2), 215–230.

Logan, J., Oakley, D., & Stowell, J. (2008). School segregation in metropolitan regions, 1970–2000: The impacts of policy choices on public education. *The American Journal of Sociology, 113*(6), 1611–1644.

Lowenhaupt, R. (2016). Immigrant acculturation in suburban schools serving the new Latino diaspora. *Peabody Journal of Education, 91*(3), 348–365.

Massey, D. S., & Mullan, B. P. (1984). Process of Black and Hispanic spatial assimilation. *American Journal of Sociology, 89*(4), 836–873.

Mickelson, R. A., & Nkomo, M. (2012). Integrated schooling, life-course outcomes, and social cohesion in multiethnic democratic societies. *Review of Research in Education, 36*(1), 197–238.

Milliken v. Bradley, 418 U.S. 717. (1974).

Monkkonen, E. H. (1980). *America becomes urban: The development of U.S. cities and towns 1780–1980.* Berkeley, CA: University of California Press.

Monroe, C. R. (2009). Teachers closing the discipline gap in an urban middle school. *Urban Education, 44*(3), 322–347.

National Center for Education Statistics (NCES) (n.d.). *Elementary/secondary information system table generator.* Retrieved from https://nces.ed.gov/ccd/elsi/tableGenerator.aspx

Oakes, J. (1995). Two cities' tracking and within-school segregation. *The Teachers College Record, 96*(4), 681–690.

Orfield, G., & Frankenberg, E. (2014). Increasingly segregated and unequal schools as courts reverse policy. *Educational Administration Quarterly, 50*(5), 718–734.

Orfield, M., & Luce, T. (2012). *America's racially diverse suburbs: Opportunities and challenges.* Minneapolis, MN: Institute on Metropolitan Opportunity, University of Minnesota.

Reardon, S. F., & Yun, J. T. (2002). Integrating neighborhoods, segregating schools: The retreat from school desegregation in the South, 1990–2000. *North Carolina Law Review, 81*(4), 1563–1596.

Rothstein, R. (2015, April 29). From Ferguson to Baltimore: The fruits of government-sponsored segregation. [Web log comment.] Retrieved from http://www.epi.org/blog/from-ferguson-to-baltimore-the-fruits-of-government-sponsored-segregation

Shannon, S. M., & Milian, M. (2002). Parents choose dual-language programs in Colorado: A survey. *Bilingual Research Journal, 26*(3), 681–696.

Shapiro, T. M. (2005). *The hidden cost of being African-American: How wealth perpetuates inequality*. New York, NY: Oxford University Press.

Thomas, W. P., & Collier, V. P. (1998). Two languages are better than one. *Educational Leadership, 55*(4), 23–27.

Turner, M. A., & Ross, S. L. (2005). How racial discrimination affects the search for housing. In X. D. Briggs (Ed.), *The geography of opportunity race and housing choice in metropolitan America* (pp. 81–102). Washington, DC: Brookings Institute Press.

Vasquez Heilig, J., Brown, K., & Brown, A. (2012). The illusion of inclusion: A critical race theory textual analysis of race and standards. *Harvard Educational Review, 82*(3), 403–424.

Villegas, A. M., & Lucas, T. (2002). *Educating culturally responsive teachers: A coherent approach*. Albany, NY: State University of New York Press.

Chapter Two

Race, Ethnicity, and Social Capital in the Changing Suburbs

Carl L. Bankston III and Stephen J. Caldas

- Suburban schools have been undergoing rapid demographic changes in recent years with a sharp increase in the percentages of students from minority backgrounds.
- The growing numbers of students from disadvantaged economic backgrounds, single-parent families, and recently arrived non-English-speaking families have presented challenges to suburban schools.
- The growth in disparities in social and economic capital associated with ethnicity is illustrated in two very different suburban school districts in one New York county.

When Americans think of suburban public schools, they often think in terms of White flight and socioeconomic advantage, in contrast to the concentrated disadvantages of central city schools. There is some justification for this view. "White flight" and, more broadly, "middle-class flight" since the 1970s have indeed left many urban core schools heavily segregated and dominated by low-income, minority students (Bankston & Caldas, 2015; Caldas & Bankston, 2014). Nevertheless, schools and communities in the suburbs have also been changing in ways that have far-reaching consequences for the social resources of students.

First among these changes is the rapidly shifting racial and ethnic composition of schools in the suburbs. Proportions of Black, Hispanic,[1] and Asian students have increased across the United States, including suburban settings. Second, the development of the "new destinations" phenomenon in immigration has resulted in the creation of new ethnic minority clusters around the nation. The suburbs, and their educational institutions, have become more heterogeneous than in the past. Third, suburban schools, as well as urban schools, have experienced growth in the percentages of students from family backgrounds associated with limited social capital.

In this chapter these changes will be explored at two levels. First, a general description will be given, based primarily on U.S. Census data, of relevant suburban student characteristics since 1980. Then, two individual districts will be compared within the patchwork of the contemporary educational environment in order to examine how race and ethnicity today are related to the social capital resources that pupils bring to their schools. Although these districts cannot be taken as representative of nationwide characteristics in all respects, it should be clear that the trends shared have been produced by larger national forces and reflect those forces and their consequences.

RACIAL AND ETHNIC CHANGE

The United States has been undergoing rapid changes in its racial and ethnic composition. In 2002, a census report on demographic change in the twentieth century noted that "the White population grew more slowly than every other race group in the second half of the twentieth century and for the century as a whole" (Hobbs & Stoops, 2002, p. 79). As a proportion, Whites decreased steadily since 1970, while the proportion of the population classified as Black increased slightly.

The greatest part of the expansion of American racial and ethnic minorities, though, came from Hispanics, who more than doubled in their numbers between 1980 and 2000 alone (Hobbs & Stoops, 2002). By 2015, the percentage of White non-Hispanics decreased to 62 percent. By 2045, the U.S. Census (2014) projects that White non-Hispanics will no longer constitute a majority of the population.

Because racial and ethnic minority group members tend to be younger than White non-Hispanics, these changes are even more marked in the public schools. In 1970, Whites made up 80 percent of public school students in all locations. Just thirty years later, this had decreased to 52 percent, and it is projected to decrease to 48 percent by 2021. The growing Hispanic population constitutes the greatest part of this change, increasing from only 5 percent of American students in 1970 to 23 percent by 2010 (Caldas & Bankston, 2014).

This demographic shift was not the result of changes only in urban schools. According to census data compiled from the American Community Survey (ACS), even outside the central cities, the racial and ethnic changes in suburban public schools in the twentieth and early twenty-first centuries have been dramatic (Ruggles, Genadek, Goeken, Grover, & Sobek, 2015).

While White, non-Hispanic students made up 80 percent of the public school pupils in 1970, they dropped to 55 percent in 2014. They had decreased over 25 percentage points in forty-four years. Black students made up more of those in suburban public schools, growing from just over 8 percent to 13 percent during the same period. As in the nation at large, Hispanics showed the most impressive growth, from under 8 percent to 23 percent.

Clearly, the great demographic changes of American schools have taken place in the suburbs, as well as in the city. Why do these trends matter, though? If young people were simply units to be educated, then it would not matter what their backgrounds or complexions might be. But students come to schools with widely varying backgrounds and from differing social environments, and these backgrounds and environments greatly affect how they will interact with their teachers and fellow students. One big background difference is economic.

According to the data extracted from the ACS, Blacks and Hispanics, as aggregates, came from suburban households with incomes only a little more than half those of Whites and Asians (Ruggles et al., 2015), with Asian families earning the most. Thus, the fastest growing minority populations in the suburbs come from demographic categories with the lowest incomes.

Moreover, the median incomes only indicate the midpoints. Approximately 16 percent of all suburban public school students, or more than one out of every six, lived in households at or below the poverty level in 2014 (Ruggles et al., 2015). This figure raises some questions about whether an increase in poverty was a long-term trend or a feature of the economic situation following the 2008 downturn. The proportion of suburban pupils below the poverty level went up only slightly from 1980 to 1990 and then continued at about 11 percent in both 1990 and 2000. There was an approximately 40 percent increase in the percentage of poor students in suburban schools between 1980 and 2014.

Students at or below the poverty level, further, tend to come from those categories that have been rising in representation. Two-thirds of suburban public school students in 2014 who were at or below the poverty level were minority group members, mostly Blacks and Hispanics (Ruggles et al., 2015). One should keep in mind that this is a very strict measure of economic limitation. The term *low income* frequently includes those somewhat above the official poverty level.

The racial and ethnic changes in schools outside the central cities, then, are more than just a shift in the ancestral origins of institutional populations. This change is an expansion of members of groups who tend to struggle against challenges and struggle under disadvantages. Many of those challenges and disadvantages are economic: comparatively low average incomes and comparatively high poverty rates. However, in the next two sections, it will be argued that the young people in these groups also face problems due to limitations of social resources, or social capital.

NEW IMMIGRANT DESTINATIONS AND YOUTH IN THE SUBURBS

Since the 1970s, the United States has been experiencing the largest wave of immigration in the nation's history. Sheer numbers of immigrants have greatly surpassed those of the great wave of a century earlier. Even as a percentage of the country's population, the proportion of residents who are foreign-born has begun to edge past that of the early twentieth century (Zhou & Bankston, 2016). The largest part of this new wave of immigrants has been arriving from Latin America, chiefly Mexico and Central America. The arrivals from Latin American constitute a new working class, heavily concentrated in jobs at the bottom of the labor force, in manual, low-paying occupations (Massey, 2008).

The new Latin American working class spread out to locations that received few immigrants earlier in American history. Although older urban concentrations continued to pull in immigrants, the jobs attracting them, including those of the new Latin American working class, appeared more and more in the suburbs. As sociologist John Logan (2007) wrote of settlement patterns in the early twenty-first century:

> Suburbs today are the location not only of agricultural and gardening industries on the periphery, but also of most job development in metropolitan regions. At the same time, the composition of the suburban housing stock has shifted (with apartment development in some places and deteriorated housing in others) and suburbs currently offer a much wider range of housing types and prices than they did before. . . . For both [Hispanics and Asians] . . . there was considerable growth in the cities, but even stronger increase in the suburbs. (p. 90)

The "Hispanic Explosion" has changed the demographic composition of schools in the suburbs, as well as in the cities. Because many suburbs or neighborhoods within suburbs have become sites of largely Hispanic communities, this means that places of settlement have made de facto school segregation by Hispanic ethnicity, as well as by race, a reality of suburban public schools. As observed in earlier work, ethnic concentration has brought problems (Bankston, 2014; Bankston & Caldas, 2015; Caldas & Bankston, 2014).

In interviews conducted with teachers in schools located in the suburban neighborhoods outside of the city of New Orleans, where the immigrants to that metropolitan area have concentrated, the teachers repeatedly said that one of their greatest pedagogical challenges was the nomadic tendency of their Latin American students. The teachers stated that new students were constantly arriving. But they also insisted that students were constantly leaving the district and that students told the teachers they would be leaving because their families were following their fathers to other locations in the quest for work (Bankston, 2014).

One of the challenges that these fluid new populations have brought to the suburbs is that of educating larger numbers of students from families with home languages other than English. In 1980, only 2 percent of suburban pupils came from families without a head who had a strong command of English. By 2014, though, this had increased to about one out of every fourteen students (Ruggles et al., 2015).

Beyond new language challenges, though, the shifting student population has brought other problems. Although Hispanic dropout rates have been declining since 2000, they remain much higher than those of other major demographic groups (Bankston, 2014). In addition, Hispanic students show much lower average outcomes than White and Asian students on all indicators of academic achievement, including major achievement tests, college entrance tests, and grade-point averages (Bankston & Caldas, 2015; Caldas & Bankston, 2014). Part of the Hispanic disadvantage is undoubtedly purely economic. But they also show disadvantages in social capital.

The socioeconomic position of Hispanics in the United States endows them not only with lower income than most non-Hispanics but also with fewer social resources. Suárez-Orozco (1987) and Matute-Bianchi (1986; 1991) have described the outlooks of Mexican American teenagers as consequences of generations of discrimination and isolation. In contrast to members of more recently arrived groups, the information about chances for life improvement that moves through their network lines is about barriers, not paths, to opportunity.

The settlement of new groups of people in the suburbs, especially Hispanics, has been part of the social capital deficit in the changing suburbs. This growing minority school population has also tended to show the greatest limitations in the kinds of social resources that contribute heavily to success in American schools. In the following section, how variations in social resources are linked to the shifted racial and ethnic composition of suburban schools is closely explored.

FAMILY BACKGROUNDS AND SOCIAL CAPITAL

The term *social capital* refers to the idea that relationships among people may be assets that can produce favorable outcomes for those involved in the relationships (Bankston, 2014). The sociologist James S. Coleman developed one of the most influential sociological approaches to social capital. In *Foundations of Social Theory* (1990), Coleman defines *social capital* in terms of network closure. Social capital exists, in Coleman's view, when there are close and closed networks among a set of individuals, promoting advantageous behavior.

Coleman's work identified three primary parts to the generation of social capital. First, there are established patterns of interactions among persons. These are conceived in terms of network relations, which may occur within formal institutions such as the family or the school, or in less formally structured settings such as the neighborhood. Second, there are normative orientations produced and maintained by patterns of interactions. Third, there are behavioral outcomes. Relationships among persons qualify as social capital when they produce and maintain normative orientations that lead to behavioral outcomes that enable individuals and groups to achieve desired goals.

Family, the earliest and most immediate influence on the lives of young people, lies at the heart of Coleman's concept of social capital. Caldas and Bankston (2014) reported family variations in measurable social resources across racial and ethnic groups. Black children in the critical age group of three to five, for example, were substantially less likely to be read to by their parents than either White or Asian children. Hispanic children in this age group were by far the least likely to enjoy the experience of being read to by parents.

Family structure is an especially important source of social capital, although not the only source. Other things being equal, children in two-parent families have an advantage over children in one-parent families. The former provides more control and direction to children than the latter. Family structure is also linked to social capital at the community, peer, and institutional levels. Communities, youth peer groups, and schools based on single-parent families concentrate and intensify family disadvantages (see findings in Bankston & Caldas, 1998; Bankston & Caldas, 2000; Caldas & Bankston, 1998; Caldas & Bankston, 1999).

Researchers have generally found that, even controlling for economic situations, children from single-parent families are more likely than other children to engage in substance abuse, to display aggressive or violent behavior, and to suffer from a variety of psychological problems. Students from one-parent families also show a greater tendency to display behaviors and attitudes toward school that result in poor school performance (McLanahan & Booth, 1989; Sun & Li, 2011; Vaden-Kiernan, Ialongo, Pearson, & Kellam, 1995).

While single-parent families in general provide less advantageous settings for generating social capital, children living with never-married mothers face the greatest difficulties, even apart from the fact that these children face much greater risk of poverty than those in other types of families. Relative instability and general social marginality frequently plague unmarried families. The schools that teach children from these families, in turn, reflect the instability and marginality.

Family background is a particular challenge for schools serving minority students. Single-parent families in general and never-married families in particular have risen sharply in the Black and Hispanic populations, compared to White or Asian populations. By 2012, 72 percent of African American children were born to single mothers and only 35 percent of school-age African American children lived in two-parent families. Hispanics, whose rapid population growth owed to immigration, showed trends in family structure similar to those of African Americans.

Percentages of Hispanic children born to single mothers increased from one-quarter in 1982 to over 53 percent in 2012. By contrast, 30 percent of White children and 17 percent of Asian children were born to single mothers in 2012. While school-age Hispanic children were more likely than African American children to live in two-parent families (about 62 percent of Hispanic children lived in married couple households), school-age Hispanics were far less likely than either White children or Asian children to live in a married couple household (Caldas & Bankston, 2014; Zhou & Bankston, 2016).

These changes in family structure are also seen among suburban students. According to the data compiled from the ACS, the percentages of suburban public school students in married couple families decreased steadily among all racial and ethnic groups from 1980 through 2014 (Ruggles et al., 2015). However, the decrease was greatest among Black and Hispanic families.

The biggest decrease was among suburban Black pupils, with only a minority living in households with two parents (42.6 percent). Both Hispanic and Asian suburban students were less likely than White non-Hispanics to live with two parents, but differences were not great. Simply looking at marital status of parents, then, the growing family structure disadvantage appears to be an issue facing Black students more than all others.

Looking at the even greater problem of never-married mothers, though, variations appear much greater. The trend toward enrollees in suburban public schools living with mothers who have never married also grew, but most sharply among Blacks, and after 2000, Hispanics as well. In 1980, fewer than 10 percent of Black students and only 2 percent of Hispanic students in the suburbs were in households with mothers who had never married. By 2014, this had increased to 30 percent and 13 percent, respectively.

One should keep in mind that these figures are a series of "snapshots." They show only family settings at particular points in time, not percentages of students who have ever lived in single-parent families or who were born to single mothers who later acquired spouses. To the extent that family structure changes indicate growing social capital deficiencies linked to demographic changes, then, the problem is greater than these figures show.

A STUDY IN CONTRASTS IN
WESTCHESTER COUNTY, NEW YORK

An example of the enormous and growing racial and ethnic disparities in social and economic capital in suburban America exists in Westchester County, New York. In the aggregate, this suburban bedroom community to New York City appears very wealthy. It is home to successful investment bankers, CEOs of major multinational corporations, and well-known American presidential families. Many of these titans of American finance, business, and politics commute to nearby Manhattan (or Washington) to conduct their business. The county's residents pay some of the highest property taxes in the country, and the average per-pupil spending in its forty or so public school districts is approximately double the national average (Campbell, 2015).

However, there are two Westchesters: the mostly White (and increasingly Asian), privileged one with manicured lawns and horse farms on large estates, and the other, with a large proportion of mostly working-class and poor Hispanics who provide the steady stream of laborers who manicure those lawns and clean the stables. These two "suburban" Westchesters live side-by-side, but could not be further apart in terms of quality of education, income, health care, social capital resources, and any number of other quality-of-life outcomes.

On the one hand there are communities like the city of Rye, with an overwhelmingly White population, which according to the ACS (U.S. Census, 2016) had a median household income in 2014 of $155,422. On the other there are communities like the Village of Port Chester, which shares a political boundary with Rye, where almost two-thirds of the community is Hispanic and the median income is roughly a third of next-door Rye.

Port Chester, New York

The Village of Port Chester is located in the southern part of Westchester, on the shore of the Long Island Sound (Baker, 2013). Port Chester, which is a short twenty-mile commute to nearby New York City, was originally a small community of predominantly Italian, Irish, and Jewish immigrants to the United States (Chen, 2001). However, the racial and ethnic composition of the community began to change rapidly with the large influx of Hispanic immigrants from Latin America, which first started in the early 1960s with Cubans, followed by a wave of immigration from all over Latin America beginning in the 1990s.

By 2000, Port Chester had become the first Westchester County community to have a plurality of Hispanic residents, when 46 percent of the village population identified as Hispanic (Chen, 2001). By 2010, almost 60 percent of Port Chester's population was Hispanic (U.S. Census, 2010), a percentage estimated to have crept up to 61 percent by 2014 (U.S. Census, 2016). The census estimated that 64 percent of the population spoke a language other than English at home, and only 69 percent of adults had a high school diploma with only 21 percent having a bachelor's degree or higher. Median household income in Port Chester was $56,134, with 14.5 percent of persons living in poverty.

While the median value of $441,000 for a home in Port Chester may seem high, it is less than half that of its affluent Rye neighbor. Also, many Hispanic families in Port Chester crowd together in rented rooms in subdivided single family homes (Chen, 2001). And as for crowding, with a 2010 population density of 12,500 persons per square mile, the 2.5 square mile village much more resembles an urban streetscape than a sleepy suburban bedroom community. Though majority Hispanic, the village had only one Hispanic on its board of six village trustees. Additionally, almost one-third of Port Chester residents did not have health insurance, including 7.8 percent of its children.

On the K–12 education front, during the 2014–2015 school year, English learners (ELs) constituted one-quarter of the entire student population, and 72 percent of all Port Chester's public school students were classified as economically disadvantaged (New York State Education Department, 2016). However, by national standards, the Port Chester schools are very well funded. According to the National Center for Educational Statistics (NCES) (2016), in the 2011–2012 school year, per-pupil spending in the school district was $19,863 (in 2014 adjusted dollars), a figure that was near the New York State average, and 45 percent higher than the national average of $11,000.

Educational outcomes in Port Chester, however, were much lower than New York State in general, and lower still when compared to the neighboring Rye city school district. On the 2015 grades 3–8 English language arts (ELA) state assessment, only 19 percent of the district's students scored at the "Proficient" level. Only 15 percent of the district's Hispanic students scored "Proficient" (New York State Education Department, 2016).

Whites scored much better (34 percent), and Blacks scored worse (13 percent), but even these two racial categories scored lower than the state average for these groups (40 percent and 18 percent, respectively). Results were similarly poor on the grades 3–8 math assessment, with only 20 percent of Port Chester's students scoring at the "Proficient" level in this subject. The graduation rate for Port Chester students in 2015 was 81 percent (84 percent for Hispanics) (New York State Education Department, 2016).

City of Rye, New York

The contrast between Port Chester and its adjacent sister city of Rye could not be starker. Rye, too, is a suburban bedroom community of New York City, with an estimated 2010 population of 15,720. With a population density roughly one-fifth that of Port Chester, the city of Rye is ironically more like the village, and Port Chester is more like the city. The percent of the population identifying as White alone was almost 90 percent, with only 6.5 percent of the population identifying as Hispanic. Only 20 percent of persons spoke a language other than English at home.

In regards to education levels, fully 97 percent of Rye's adult population had a high school diploma, with a remarkable 74 percent having a bachelor's degree or higher (almost four times the rate of Port Chester). The median income of Rye adults was estimated at $155,422, with a poverty rate of only 3.4 percent (U.S. Census, 2016). The average value of a home in Rye was over a million dollars. Only 4.4 percent of all persons and 0.9 percent of children under eighteen were estimated to not have health insurance, rates from seven to fourteen times lower than those of Port Chester residents.

Shifting to K–12 education, the disparities between Port Chester and Rye are just as huge as those noted in the other social and economic indicators. On the grades 3–8 ELA state test, 61 percent of Rye students were deemed at the "Proficient" level, compared to 19 percent in Port Chester. However, Hispanic students in Rye schools passed the ELA state test at rates three times higher than their counterparts in Port Chester, with 43 percent attaining proficiency on the state ELA test (compared to only 15 percent of Hispanic students in Port Chester). White students in Rye schools attained proficiency on the ELA tests at almost twice the rate of Port Chester Whites (61 percent compared to 34 percent), and Blacks scored proficient at rates more than three times their homologues in Port Chester (43 percent compared to 13 percent).

These markedly differing test score results among the same racial/ethnic groups in the two communities suggest vastly different social capital resources and climate between the two school districts and communities in which the schools are embedded. Asians, of which there were too few in Port Chester for reporting test results, scored the highest of all racial/ethnic categories in Rye, attaining a 72 percent proficiency level on the ELA test. The state math test results followed a similar pattern by race and ethnicity. The graduation rate for Rye students in 2015 was 96 percent (compared to 81 percent in Port Chester) (New York State Education Department, 2016).

Importantly, as good as the academic outcomes are for students in Rye City public schools, fully 34 percent of all students in Rye are not even enrolled in the public schools, but rather opt for a private school education (U.S. Census, 2016). This is almost twice the 18 percent of all K–12 Port

Chester students who are enrolled in private schools. In most of the United States, private school enrollments are high where public school performance is low (Caldas & Bankston, 2014; Bankston & Caldas, 2015). The Rye pattern is suggestive of just how wealthy and exclusive the population of Rye is because parents choose to invest in a pricey private school education when a high-quality public alternative is available.

REASONS FOR THE GULF

What can account for such a gulf in the economic, social, health, and education outcomes of two suburban communities in one of the richest counties in the United States separated by no more than a line on a map? Clearly, public spending in education is almost certainly not an important explanatory factor. In 2011–2012, the Rye schools spent only 9.6 percent more per student ($21,974) than did Port Chester schools, even though the Rye residents were in general much wealthier. By contrast, though, Rye students attained proficiency on state tests at a rate from three to four times higher than their Port Chester counterparts.

Moreover, the per-pupil spending figure does not capture much additional investment in the Port Chester schools by private aid agencies and a local private college that has designated several Port Chester schools as intensive professional development (PD) sites for its teacher candidates. These "PD" schools offer much on-site professional expertise and in-service training by doctoral-holding educational specialists and teacher interns (Wepner et al., 2012). Also, two Port Chester elementary schools are full-service "community schools," offering health and other social and educational services on-site for students and their parents. These same services are not offered in any of Rye's schools.

Can a lack of English proficiency possibly account for the large differences in educational outcomes between the students in these two communities? After all, at least three-quarters of Port Chester's students are Hispanic, one-quarter are ELs, and almost two-thirds of all residents speak a language other than English at home. Perhaps even Hispanic students who are no longer classified as ELs have not attained a mastery of English that would allow them to compete academically with native English speakers. Even fluent English-speaking Port Chester students might not be exposed to as much English in their homes and communities as students in all-English environments.

On closer examination, however, the "language deficiency" argument as an explanation for poor educational outcomes does not hold up well in our comparison. First of all, both Black and White Port Chester students scored at proficiency levels ranging from two to three times lower than did Rye

Blacks and Whites, and we can safely assume that the vast majority of these students are native speakers of English living in all English-speaking home environments.

Secondly, even among ELs there was a huge discrepancy in testing outcomes between the two districts. ELs in Port Chester attained proficiency on the state ELA and math tests at rates of 4 and 8 percent, respectively. This contrasts sharply with the performance of ELs in Rye, who attained proficiency on these same two tests at levels of 64 and 62 percent!

These astounding figures, particularly the proficiency of Rye ELs on the ELA test, are worth reflection. What the data clearly indicate is that ELs (i.e., students not yet officially proficient in English) in Rye attained proficiency on a test that measures ELA skills at a level almost twice that of White students in Port Chester for whom English is a first language. Moreover, this rate is almost five times higher than that of Black Port Chester students. It seems the English deficiency explanation is not a strong one. If anything, it would be easier to argue that native English proficiency does not seem to matter at all on a test of ELA, as counterintuitive as this would seem.

As pointed out in this chapter, these glaring differences in educational outcomes between two adjacent suburban communities are a direct consequence of differences in the funds of economic and social capital available to the students in these two very different social environments. The discrepant economic, social, health, and educational indices that we shared for Port Chester and Rye are all proxies for very tangible social capital resources. In short, the traditional disadvantages of urban-dwelling minority groups in America seem to have followed these students to the suburbs, as both our macro and micro analyses have demonstrated.

A CLOSER LOOK AT TWO VERY DIFFERENT COMMUNITIES

The census data itself describe two very different social environments in which the children of Port Chester and Rye are being raised. These social environments embed the children of these two communities in very different social networks, through which norms, information, and culture are transmitted. The differences are obvious at the most basic level—the family. In Rye, 65.1 percent of persons aged 15 or older were married, compared to only 45.1 percent of the comparable Port Chester population. This discrepancy suggests an overall higher level of community stability.

Moreover, something about the qualities of these family structures from an analysis of occupation structure of the two communities, in terms of the most common types of employment, is known. In 2015, an estimated 61 percent of Rye adults were employed in management, business, science, and arts occupations, compared to only 22 percent of Port Chester adults, who were much more heavily represented in the service (22 percent in Port Chester vs. 8.6 percent in Rye) and construction/maintenance (10.5 percent vs. 2.5 percent) occupations (U.S. Census, 2016). Thus, children in Rye were more likely to be in families headed by professionals and the social and financial resources these professionals could provide.

Something is also known about the social order present in these two communities by looking at crime statistics. Higher crime rates would suggest higher levels of fear and distrust among citizens. In Rye the crime rate in 2014 was 21.8 crimes per 100,000 persons. This compares to the national average of 284.1. While Port Chester's crime rate of 138.4 was significantly lower than the national average, it was still six times higher than Rye City's, and more comparable to an urban environment. In short, with a crime rate thirteen times lower than the national average, Rye City was clearly a community where citizens felt safe and secure, and where social trust was high.

To sum up, two adjacent suburban communities in one of the wealthiest areas of the country are vastly different in terms of a variety of economic, education, and social outcomes. The one, with a high minority, particularly Hispanic concentration, more closely resembles an urban city center, while the other, overwhelmingly White, fits the popular conception of a prosperous, leafy bedroom community.

This bifurcated reality is a microcosm of how suburban America in the twenty-first century is very much a perpetuation of the racial, economic, and class segregation that characterized urban America in the twentieth century.

CONCLUSION

Suburban public schools have been going through rapid changes in student populations in recent years. These changes have affected both the social and economic assets students bring with them to schools. Although urban centers tend to have the densest concentration of minority students, suburban schools have experienced a sharp increase in percentages of students from racial and ethnic minorities. The "new destinations" phenomenon, the tendency of immigrants to move to locations that previously received few immigrants, has meant that children from immigrant families make up a large and growing part of the suburban student population.

A number of major disadvantages characterize the new suburban school populations. Black and Hispanic students tend to come from families of lower socioeconomic status than those of non-Hispanic White students. One of the most notable sources of disadvantage, in terms of social capital, lies in family structure. Black and Hispanic students are far more likely than others to come from single-parent families, particularly never-married-mother families.

Those concerned with educational opportunity should consider how opportunity is affected by changes in the suburbs, and by differences among school populations in the suburbs, as well as by differences between urban and suburban schools. This chapter presents an example of suburban schools in one geographic area of the Northeast, to illustrate how demographic change, produced mainly by immigration, has produced variations in school settings for students in neighboring districts.

Although the area in this example has some unique characteristics, such as proximity to New York City and relatively high median incomes, it illustrates how the social capital endowments of today's suburban students are connected to educational outcomes in schools. The big dividing line among schools in the suburbs is created by the demographic composition of those schools.

REFLECTION QUESTIONS

1. Why are the student populations of suburban public schools changing?
2. How are the advantages and disadvantages that students from different backgrounds bring with them to schools connected to advantages and disadvantages in American society in general?
3. What policies could lawmakers or educational administrators enact that might realistically improve educational opportunities in changing public schools?

NOTE

1. We use the term *Hispanic* throughout this chapter to refer to individuals also referred to as Latino.

REFERENCES

Baker, A. (2013, July 20). Town's schools test a law of racial arithmetic. *New York Times,* p. A1.
Bankston, C. L. (2014). *Immigrant networks and social capital.* London, UK: Polity Press.
Bankston, C. L., & Caldas, S. J. (1998). Family structure, schoolmates, and the racial inequalities of schools. *Journal of Marriage and the Family, 60*(3), 715–723.
Bankston, C. L., & Caldas, S. J. (2000). Majority African American schools and the family structures of schools: School racial composition and academic achievement among Black and White students. *Sociological Focus, 33*(3), 243–263.
Bankston, C. L., & Caldas, S. J. (2015). *Controls and choices: The educational marketplace and the failure of school desegregation.* Lanham, MD: Rowman & Littlefield.
Caldas, S. J., & Bankston, C. L. (1998). Female-headed families and school environments: Does the family structure of schoolmates make a difference in academic achievement? *Louisiana Education Research Journal, 23*(1), 101–128.

Caldas, S. J., & Bankston, C. L. (1999). A multilevel examination of student, school, and district level effects on student achievement. *Journal of Educational Research, 93*(2), 91–100.

Caldas, S. J., & Bankston, C. L. (2014). *Still failing: The continuing paradox of school desegregation.* Lanham, MD: Rowman & Littlefield.

Campbell, J. (2015, September 15). Report: NY spent $21K per pupil in 2013–14. *The Journal News.* Retrieved from http://www.lohud.com/story/news/education/2015/09/14/report-ny-spent-per-pupil/72256554

Chen, D. W. (2001, April 13). Hispanic influx slowly altering a town veneer. *New York Times,* p. B3.

Coleman, J. S. (1990). *Foundations of social theory.* Cambridge, MA: Belknap Press of Harvard University Press.

Hobbs, F., & Stoops, N. (2002). *Demographic trends in the twentieth century* (Census 2000 Special Reports, Series CENSR-4). Washington, DC: U.S. Government Printing Office.

Logan, J. (2007). Settlement patterns in metropolitan America. In M. C. Waters & R. Ueda with H. B. Marrow (Eds.), *The new Americans: A guide to immigration since 1965* (pp. 83–97). Cambridge, MA: Harvard University Press.

Massey, D. S. (2008). *Categorically unequal: The American stratification system.* New York, NY: Russell Sage Foundation.

Matute-Bianchi, M. E. (1986). Ethnic identities and patterns of school success and failure among Mexican-descent and Japanese American students in a California high school: An ethnographic analysis. *American Journal of Education, 95*(1), 233–255.

Matute-Bianchi, M. E. (1991). Situational ethnicity and patterns of school performance among immigrant and non-immigrant Mexican-descent students. In M. A. Gibson & J. U. Ogbu (Eds.), *Minority status and schooling: A comparative study of immigrant and involuntary minorities* (pp. 205–247). New York, NY: Garland.

McLanahan, S., & Booth, K. (1989). Mother-only families: Problems, prospects, and politics. *Journal of Marriage and the Family, 51*(3), 557–579.

National Center for Education Statistics. (2016). Retrieved from http://nces.ed.gov/ccd/districtsearch/district_detail.asp?ID2=3623460

New York State Education Department. (2016). *School Report Cards.* Retrieved from http://www.data.nysed.org

Ruggles, S., Genadek, K., Goeken, R., Grover, J., & Sobek, M. (2015). *Integrated public use microdata series: Version 6.0* [Machine-readable database] (includes American Community Survey data). Minneapolis, MN: University of Minnesota.

Suárez-Orozco, M. (1987). Toward a psychosocial understanding of Hispanic adaptation to American schooling. In H. Trueba (Ed.), *Success or failure? Learning and the languages of minority students* (pp. 156–168). New York, NY: Newbury House.

Sun, Y., & Li, Y. (2011). Effects of family structure type and stability on children's academic performance trajectories. *Journal of Marriage and the Family, 73*(3), 541–556.

U.S. Census. (2010). *Community facts.* Retrieved from http://factfinder.census.gov/faces/tableservices/jsf/pages/productview.xhtml?src=CF

U.S. Census. (2014). *Population projections.* Table 11. Retrieved from http://www.census.gov/population/projections/data/national/2014/summarytables.html

U.S. Census. (2016). American Community Survey data for Port Chester Village. Retrieved from http://factfinder.census.gov

Vaden-Kiernan, N., Ialongo, N. S., Pearson, J., & Kellam, S. (1995) Household family structure and children's aggressive behavior: A longitudinal study of urban elementary school children. *Journal of Abnormal Child Psychology, 23*(5), 553–568.

Wepner, S., Ferrara, J., Rainville, K. N., Gómez, D. W., Lang, D. E., & Bigaouette, L. (2012). *Changing suburbs, changing students: Helping school leaders face challenges.* New York, NY: Corwin.

Zhou, M., & Bankston, C. L. (2016). *The rise of the new second generation.* Cambridge, UK: Polity Press.

Chapter Three

Administrators' Accountabilities in Changing Suburban Schools

Shelley B. Wepner and Diane W. Gómez

- School district and school-based administrators have a unique set of political, fiscal, educational, and community pressures because of the competing forces and ever-changing nature of the student population.
- Administrators are constantly held accountable and must demonstrate in their changing suburban schools and districts that they are closing the achievement gap.
- Administrators in changing suburban districts can and should pursue various organizational structures, programs, and professional development opportunities for their stakeholders.

Rockport School District epitomizes a changing suburban school district. Located in an upper suburb of a major metropolitan city in the northeast part of the United States, Rockport has five K–5 elementary schools, one middle school, and one high school. The elementary schools are "neighborhood" schools, whereas the middle school and high school draw from all over the district.

Three of the neighborhood schools continue to have children of primarily White, upper-middle-class and lower-upper-class parents who represent the business, arts, and sports industries. Two of the elementary schools have seen significant diversity influence the composition of the schools, with increasing numbers of English learners (ELs) who are living in poverty.

The district's report card score dropped from an "A" to a "B" because the once-high four-year college acceptance rate to the most prestigious institutions fell considerably as a result of the high concentration of minority students who are barely graduating, pursuing vocations, or enrolling in two-year community colleges. The mainstream culture and climate of the school district have shifted from pride and acceptance to confusion and anger because of the downgrade of the district's reputation.

The district superintendent's accountability as an effective administrator has been called into question. As the district superintendent for fifteen years, Dr. John Cashen has enjoyed his status as a fair-minded, compassionate, strategic, and successful leader who changed the landscape of the professional staff, developed and implemented new program initiatives, and focused on all aspects of the students' development. His political capital with parents has been high because of his focus on high-quality instruction (Daresh & Aplin, 2001; Erwin, Winn, Gentry, & Cauble, 2010; Wepner et al., 2012).

Lately, his elected school board, still comprised primarily of White wealth, is criticizing him for wanting to remove funds from existing programs to support bilingual education and professional development programs for teachers to learn new instructional strategies for working with a diverse student population (Bernstein, 2004). School board members, reflecting the White parent community, see him as too concerned about the "brown" children's success and not focused enough on ensuring that the "White" children continue to compete nationally for the coveted spots at ivy-league schools.

In contrast, and to contribute to the conflict, parents of minority children are beginning to express their dismay through a newly formed Parent Teacher Association (PTA) of Hispanic parents. The Hispanic parents now have biweekly meetings, and have used these meetings to develop a list of grievances against Dr. Cashen, focused mainly on his lack of success in funding programs that will help their children succeed in school.

Dr. Cashen's principals and teachers are questioning his ability to handle the competing forces of the community while making the necessary district-wide changes to help with the achievement gap, which they acknowledge is about race and class. His principals and teachers are very concerned about standardized test score differences, dropout rates, advanced placement exam results, and college acceptance rates (Ladson-Billings, 2006).

As Dr. Cashen's internal and external stakeholders are questioning his leadership, he too is worried about his agility and fortitude for bringing together his district to address the many challenges that confront them as a result of this demographic shift. He knows that he needs to honor his community's history while bringing the entire district together into this new era of multicultural coexistence (Wepner et al., 2012).

He also has learned through his local and national networks that he must be the one to work with his district's communities and constituents to institute changes that will shift the political power, alter core values and beliefs, and invest in new programs and resources for minority students (Holme, Diem, & Welton, 2013).

FACTORS THAT AFFECT SCHOOL DISTRICT ADMINISTRATORS' ACCOUNTABILITY

School district administrators are judged, first and foremost, by their students' achievements. Administrators depend on their teaching and administrative staff to create learning environments that promote students' intellectual, emotional, social, and ethical growth. Historically, school district administrators or superintendents of schools have faced different sets of challenges and opportunities in urban, suburban, and rural school districts, with notable student achievement differences. Whereas urban and rural school administrators celebrate when fewer students drop out of school, suburban administrators boast about an increased number of merit finalists and prestigious four-year college acceptances.

The changing suburban school district phenomenon has changed the dialogue for administrators and their accountability about what constitutes student achievement. Changing suburban school district administrators must now change the formula for determining success to account for four critical variables: (1) changing student population; (2) changing parent population; (3) an achievement gap; and (4) changing expectations for teacher performance.

These variables must be considered within the context of changing government rules and regulations, financial exigencies, competing agendas within the community, and low teacher morale from low performance ratings.

Government Mandate Pressures

Federally mandated high-stakes testing seems to have a permanent place in the educational landscape for determining students' success in U.S. schools. National standards have been developed to provide a framework for determining how students should be instructed and assessed.

Although these standards and accompanying testing protocols have been questioned for their fairness across races and cultures, they nevertheless continue to drive instructional practices (Ravitch, 2016). Federal laws affect state laws, which determine district mandates for how and when students are assessed in core academic areas, and how these tests are used. School district administrators understand that these state-required testing expectations are non-negotiable. They also recognize that such regulations are not sympathetic to teachers, administrators, or students from diverse backgrounds.

Administrators in changing suburban school districts have accepted that their standardized test scores have declined over time because of the changing nature of the students enrolled in their schools. Like a slow, imperceptible tire leak that eventually leads to a flat tire, standardized test scores decline slowly enough to go unnoticed until there is an unmistakable achievement gap between the privileged and less privileged that must be addressed, especially when such tests are tied to state and federal funding, and teachers' continued employment.

Fiscal Pressures

Funding is a huge challenge for changing suburban school districts. Government funding does not reflect the challenges districts encounter from demographic shifts (Bernstein, 2004). There also are local funding challenges, especially if there is a state-imposed tax cap. A tax cap places an upper limit on the amount of government tax a person might be required to pay. Tax caps limit the amount of funds that can go toward school budgets.

With or without tax caps, lack of support from local residents to vote for the district budget restricts spending opportunities for the schools. Homeowners who can afford to pay taxes may or may not have children of school age. Those without children in the schools may not want to use their discretionary funds to support programs that do not affect them directly.

Those with children in the schools still may vote down budgets because proposed district budgets do not support their agendas for their own children. Parents whose children would benefit the most from budgetary requests often are not homeowners, and do not have the influence to affect voting outcomes. District-level administrators must spend inordinate amounts of time at town hall meetings and community events to convince taxpayers about the importance of voting in favor of the budget to help improve the value of their properties.

Sometimes it works and sometimes it does not because different stakeholders have difficulty appreciating others' situations and concerns, especially when it comes to paying for additional resources for residents unlike themselves.

Community Pressures

Administrators in changing suburban school districts are experiencing political whiplash from the competing and often incompatible needs and demands of different types of parent populations. Those with a history in the district often are White and mainstream. They want the resources and opportunities that existed previously. Those who are new to the district often are non-White, speak languages other than English, and are financially disadvantaged. They desire instructionally appropriate programs and materials for their children. Some newcomers, however, are undocumented immigrant parents who actually are anxious about any interaction with the schools for fear of being deported.

The communities of changing districts often lack harmony and compatibility because they can represent vastly different racial, educational, linguistic, and socioeconomic backgrounds that are incompatible (Wepner et al., 2012). The community's composition usually determines the level of involvement with the schools. Parents can vary from being overly vocal about their expectations for the schools to being disengaged with any school-related issues.

Conflict about expectations can be minimal or immensely distracting, depending on the issues. For example, a changing suburban district outside of Ohio decided to eliminate its K–8 Gifted and Talented (G&T) program in order to implement dual language programs. The parents of the students directly affected by the elimination of the G&T program took their concerns to the town's mayor, a homegrown product of the G&T program, who then put pressure on the school board to reinstate the program. The superintendent was so angry and demoralized by the school board's reversal that he resigned as soon as he found another job.

Teacher Pressures

Teachers in changing suburban schools typically bring to their classrooms White, middle-class values. They often have limited understanding of cultural backgrounds of groups different from their own. They can be resistant to changing their attitudes toward minority students, relating to and appreciating their cultures, and developing the skills needed to teach students different from themselves (Wepner et al., 2012).

Even when teachers focus on subgroups for accountability purposes or engage in professional development activities to expand their understanding of different cultures, they nevertheless can see diversity as a "problem" or "challenge" (Holme et al., 2013; Welton, Diem, & Holme, 2013). Their core values can interfere with their ability to work effectively with students from diverse backgrounds.

Teachers also can be resistant to and incapable of making the necessary curricular, instructional, and assessment changes that support specific subpopulations of students. Their participation in professional development opportunities and implementation of new instructional techniques can be quite superficial because they do not really see the necessity to change the way they teach. Their opposition to change turns to disappointment when their students' once-high standardized test scores and their own teacher performance ratings are significantly lower, creating morale problems for those teachers primarily responsible for students with learning challenges.

School district administrators need to work with their administrative teams to develop a culture that communicates to their teachers their understanding of their frustrations, yet helps them change their attitudes, beliefs, expectations, and practices so that they help the students rather than blame them and their families for gaps in academic achievement (Howard, 2007).

At the same time, school district administrators need to provide comprehensive and sustainable professional development programs that prepare teachers to teach ELs. A small study of elementary school teachers found that, even when teachers are intent on instructing their ELs, they do not feel prepared because their districts have not provided them with suitable preparation (Burke, 2016).

PRESSURES AND CHALLENGES FOR SCHOOL-BASED ADMINISTRATORS

Principals, as middle managers within a school district, are in similarly precarious positions as superintendents when it comes to advocating for the needs of all students. If their schools are experiencing large influxes of immigrant and transplanted minority students with critically important educational needs, principals must do everything possible to secure the needed resources and instructional opportunities.

While they have legitimate reasons to ask for special consideration in the way that resources are allocated, especially for implementing bilingual programs or specialized literacy programs, their requests are processed alongside other principals' demands for their programs and students with their own special needs. The competition for resources reflects the educational, financial, and political pressures that principals face in trying to provide appropriate learning opportunities for different types of students in their schools.

Educational Pressures

Principals are responsible for ensuring that students have teachers who know how to teach with the appropriate curriculum, methodologies, materials, organizational structures, attitudes, and professional demeanor. If any one of these variables is askew, principals need to work with their teachers to identify, implement, monitor, and sustain the appropriate changes. These changes might require the purchase of new programs and materials, individual or collaborative professional development, grade-level or school-wide meetings, or long-term coaching.

Educational pressures escalate when an ever-widening achievement gap arises as a result of a school's inability to help all students succeed. This typically puts pressure on the budget because of the need to hire additional teachers to help with bilingual education, provide intense professional development for current teachers, offer before- and after-school programs for ELs and low-achieving students, and put into place programs that support those with learning challenges.

Fiscal Pressures

Principals' financial pressures stem from unresolved educational pressures. Principals need to move funds around from their own budgets, appeal to central administration for additional funds, apply for grant opportunities, develop partnerships with local colleges or community organizations to access resources, and appeal to their local PTAs for additional monies to fund special projects. The pursuit of these options takes time, creates anxiety, and taps into a principal's political capital.

Political Pressures

Although considered middle managers within the districtwide organizational structure, principals are the CEOs of their own schools. They are responsible for the performance of their teachers and students, and must answer to their parent community about their school's performance. They receive report cards for their schools about their students' achievement and are held accountable for every facet of their school's operation.

They have internal pressure from their teachers, administrative staff, and students, and have external pressure from central administration and the parent community. As noted above, teachers are a huge source of political pressure because of their pivotal role in the education of students. They must work with the principal in adapting to a paradigm shift that accommodates a changing student and parent population.

Although usually less politically charged, and possibly more representative of a changing population, the school's administrative and custodial staff must assess their own biases, change accordingly, and work with the principal to ensure that all students are treated fairly. When principals detect biases from their staff, they need to help them change their attitudes and behaviors, or ask them to leave their positions because of their visibility with students and the parents.

While more apparent in middle schools, junior high schools, and high schools, students from minority and disadvantaged backgrounds are aware that they have lower math and reading achievement, behavioral problems, grade retention, and greater risk of interpersonal or self-directed violence (Cook, 2015). They know that their educational experiences have not been as rich as their White counterparts, and they often do not expect much success with college and career opportunities. A self-fulfilling prophecy of failure by actions on and off school grounds can create intense political pressure for principals who are trying to promote community-wide acceptance.

DEVELOPING A PLAN TO HELP WITH ACCOUNTABILITY

With an understanding that a formula does not exist to resolve the achievement gap that continues to grow in changing suburban school districts, administrators, whether at the district or school level, must show progress in addressing the many factors that can help with such disparities between advantaged and disadvantaged students. To help with this accountability, administrators need to work with their administrative teams to gather as much information as possible.

Administrators should use this information to develop a workable and realistic plan that is aligned with statewide mandates and involves the professional staff and the community, and frequently assess the value of the plan so that it can continue to evolve to incorporate unanticipated changes at the local and state levels. Information gathering leads to administrators' grasp of the demographic shifts within their districts and schools (e.g., number and type of immigrants, housing situations, previous educational backgrounds of the children and their parents, home language[s], and level of poverty).

Information gathering also helps administrators learn about funding options and opportunities from local and state governments, student assessment data, current instructional needs and opportunities, teachers' proficiencies and professional development needs, and community needs and pressures. Environmental scans such as a SWOT (strengths, weaknesses, opportunities, and threats) Analysis can help to create a portrait of the district's perceived strengths and weaknesses and an inventory of contextually based needs that can be used to create plans (Immigrate to Manitoba, Canada, n.d.; Wepner & Hopkins, 2011).

Plans provide pathways for influencing student outcomes for all students, particularly those who are racially and culturally different from the mainstream culture. Plans most likely involve changes in curriculum, instruction, assessment, programs, materials, professional development, personnel, and community relations. Inasmuch as such plans usually require additional funds, changes in the way teachers teach, and shifts in attitudes and expectations across the district and community, administrators need to be quite skillful and strategic in the way they work with their stakeholders to develop and execute plans.

Assessing the value of such plans through regular data collection offers evidence of administrators' progress in making changes that benefit students' achievement. Dramatic changes in students' standardized test scores cannot be expected; rather, indicators of steady changes with components of the plan communicate that the district is embracing what is needed to honor the population as a whole. Any and all changes should be reviewed for their value in relation to existing resources, current mandates, and short-term and long-range impact.

STRUCTURAL AND PROGRAMMATIC OPTIONS FOR ADMINISTRATORS IN CHANGING SUBURBAN SCHOOLS

Administrators can pursue several options within their plans that focus on (1) district or school organizational structures, (2) programs, and (3) professional development opportunities for teachers and staff. For some districts and schools, the implementation of change in one of the areas is sufficient to address accountability. For other changing suburban schools, a combination of initiatives from several areas is important to meet the needs of the schools and their communities. Communication with families to build support for these options is critical (Diem, Frankenberg, Cleary, & Ali, 2014).

District or School Organizational Structures

Alternate school or district structures that can increase educational equity and reduce district and school costs are the Princeton Plan for elementary schools, magnet schools, parent choice, and full-service community schools. The mission of these three different structures is to provide a level playing field for all students, not only ELs.

The Princeton Plan

The Princeton Plan was developed in Princeton, New Jersey, to desegregate its schools in 1948. More recently, the Princeton Plan has been considered a cost-saving method for elementary public schools that helps with the nation-wide expansion of property tax caps. With this plan, students of the same age are placed in one school rather than using geographic lines for placement (Fichter, 2012). For example, all kindergarteners and first graders in the district are placed in the same building. Likewise, all second and third graders are in another building, and all fourth and fifth graders are in yet another.

The advantages of the Princeton Plan are economical and educational. The Princeton Plan allows for downsizing faculty, thus reducing salary expenditures, while enhancing the educational opportunities for the students. By regrouping students by age, there is more equitable distribution of class sizes. With all teachers and staff teaching and working with the same grades and ages in a building, there is an opportunity for curriculum continuity and collegial interaction that helps school districts comply with the demands of the standards movement (Nuzzo, 2013).

There are some disadvantages to the Princeton Plan. Families with more than one child in grades kindergarten through fourth or fifth grade in the school district may encounter problems with transportation as well as drop-off and dismissal times, as their children may be in different school buildings. Transportation may be an additional financial factor for the school district to accommodate children's transportation needs to different schools that are not in their immediate neighborhood (Island Tree Schools, n.d.).

Another concern for parents and school personnel is the increased number of times a child needs to transition from one school to the next. Usually children transition from elementary school to middle school and middle school to high school. With the Princeton Plan, one or more additional school transitions occur (Island Tree Schools, n.d.).

Magnet Schools

Magnet schools are options of choice for both elementary and secondary public school districts. Instruction tends to be inquiry and performance-based and taught within the framework of the overall focus or theme of the magnet school; such as mathematics and science, world languages, and fine and performing arts. Students' interests and talents usually determine their placement in a magnet school. Generally, magnet schools do not have any entrance criteria (Magnets School of America, n.d.).

Since placement is based on student interests, the student population generally represents a wide range of cultural and socioeconomic backgrounds as well as diverse student assets. Students might represent those who are gifted, those with special needs, and those who are emergent bilinguals. As such, magnet schools strive to create a community of learners, high level cognitive learning, and transparency of curriculum (Magnet Schools of America, n.d.).

Research on magnet schools suggests that they promote racial diversity, high levels of academic achievement in reading, social studies, and mathematics, regular attendance, and high graduation rates. Additionally, magnet school teachers represent greater racial diversity and more stability than their regular public school counterparts (Siegel-Hawley & Frankenberg, 2011). While most of the research on magnet schools has been conducted in urban schools, magnet schools have become a viable option for suburban schools that have encountered a change in their student population and needs.

Montclair School District is a diverse suburban school district in the northern part of New Jersey that instituted a magnet school system in 1977 as a measure to desegregate. The magnet schools have been so successful that, in spite of transportation costs and an extensive selection process, the school board of education moved to make magnet schools a permanent structure for the district (Wirt, 2013).

As with the Princeton Plan, magnet schools place students in schools outside of their local neighborhood. White Plains School District, a suburban district outside of New York City, created a hybrid option that allows for parental input in placing their children outside of their neighborhood schools (White Plains Public School District, n.d.).

Full-Service Community School

A neighborhood-based option is a full-service community school with a set of partnerships between the school and other community resources. Its focus is on educating the whole child (Coalition of Community Schools, 2016).

There are several models of community schools, each designed with a collaborative network of community and school partners to meet the needs of the school district and its community. Changing suburban Port Chester School District in New York has seven on-site partnerships in the areas of health services, mental health services, parent advocacy, adult education, afterschool programs, university-school education, and professional development (Gómez, Ferrara, Santiago, Fanelli, & Taylor, 2012; Santiago, Ferrara, & Quinn, 2012).

The community school model draws from all members of the community, and does not educate the child in isolation. The entire school and its community become invested agents in the education of all the community's children.

Educational and Instructional Programs

Educational and instructional programs exist that promote English language development (ELD) and literacy and overall academic achievement for students who speak a language other than English at home. School districts demonstrate that they are taking responsibility when their programs match the needs of their students and families with their resources, faculty, and staff in relation to state and federal guidelines and mandates. A district's program selection will depend on its situation.

The overarching goal for all programs is for students to become academically proficient and fluent in all four English language skills: listening, speaking, reading, and writing. There are several types of language-development program options for districts to consider. Three such programs are English language instructional programs, bilingual education programs, and programs that extend beyond the traditional school day and school year.

English Language Instructional Programs

English-only programs are a viable option for schools and districts that have many home languages and cultures represented by their student population. The goal of English-only programs is to develop English literacy. In all cases the language of instruction is English. There are two basic models: (1) English as a second language (ESL)/English for Speakers of Other Languages (ESOL) push-in/pull-out, and (2) content-based programs.

In ESL/ESOL or ELD programs, students receive all or part of their instruction in the general education class. Either the students are pulled out of the classroom for English instruction provided by an ESL/ESOL specialist, or the ESL/ESOL specialist pushes into the general education classroom to provide support.

Content-based programs, such as structured English immersion (SEI) or sheltered English and Specially Designed Academic Instruction in English (SDAIE), have the common goal of teaching both English language and academic content. English instruction is adapted to students' proficiency through simplified English, manipulatives, visual aids, and gestures (Moughamian, Rivera, & Francis, 2009).

While additional first or native language (L1) support can be given separately within the content-based programs, it often is not included. English-only programs can be advantageous for schools and districts that do not have teachers and support staff who speak or are proficient in the home languages of their students.

Bilingual Instructional Programs

Bilingual instructional programs use both English and the students' home language as the languages of instruction. Despite common thought, the goal of bilingual instructional programs is for the students to become academically proficient in English, while at the same time continuing to develop their first language. Fundamental to this process is the principle that students' well-developed first language transfers to students' literacy in their second, third, or fourth language (Krashen, 2016).

In the United States, two basic bilingual programs are generally offered: transitional bilingual programs and dual language programs. In both cases, there are two languages of instruction, one being English. The programs can vary in time and intensity (Moughamian et al., 2009).

Transitional or early exit instruction can last for two or three years, and maintenance, also called developmental or late-exit bilingual, can last for six years. In both program types, native or home language is used alongside English instruction. The use of the native language varies greatly, from 50 percent in English to 50 percent in the native language, to 60–40 or 70–30. Early exit programs move students to English-only instruction quickly, and do not continue to maintain native language development (Moughamian et al., 2009).

Dual-language instructional programs, also called two-way bilingual and paired bilingual programs, provide instruction in the content areas in two languages. Unique to the dual-language program is that ideally 50 percent of the students in the group are native speakers of English and the other 50 percent are ELs with the same home language. All students in the class are second-language learners, and each language group has native-speaker models of the new language they are learning (Collier & Thomas, 2009; Moughamian et al., 2009).

Instruction in a dual-language program is taught in two languages and occurs in the curricular mainstream. Both groups of students are together during the school day, as they follow the required curriculum and alternate between the two languages. The goal is for the students to become academically proficient in both languages (Collier & Thomas, 2009).

Dual-language programs enable two groups of students to learn a second language and provide a more multicultural and multilingual districtwide environment. Unlike the transitional and maintenance bilingual programs in which ELs are isolated and segregated, dual-language programs offer sociocultural support while learning a new language. Collier and Thomas's (2009) research findings on dual-language programs purport, "English learners can fully close the achievement gap in English . . . in both their primary and in English by middle school" (p. 67).

If a district has a large number of students who speak the same home language, and also has the faculty and staff who are academically proficient to teach content-area subjects in both English and that language, one of these two bilingual program options might be suitable to help with accountability.

Extended Day and Year Programs

Programs that take place after school hours and beyond the school year can be beneficial to districts and schools attempting to close the achievement gaps of their ELs. Such programs can stand alone or be part of a community–school partnership.

Successful afterschool and summer programs for ELs provide structured homework support, employ staff who are culturally and linguistically similar to the students, and include the students' families in constructive and purposefully ways. When these programs also complement the school's regular curriculum, they help to close the achievement gap because they give ELs more experience with project-based activities and more time to complete them (Pray, 2013).

Professional Development Options for Teachers and Staff

Regardless of the type of language instruction program, the quality of the instruction is extremely important (Moughamian et al., 2009). Districts often need to provide professional development and support to the faculty and staff to implement new programs.

Successful professional development emanates from the needs of the teachers, students, and families. It is embedded in teachers' day-to-day teaching practices, and is intended to improve teachers' content-specific instructional practices with the goal of improving student learning (Darling-Hammond & McLaughlin, 1995; Hirsh, 2009; Wepner, Gómez, Cunningham, Rainville, & Kelly, 2016).

Some impactful options for professional development are study groups; coaching/mentoring by peers that is topic specific; book clubs; guided, collaborative review of student work; classroom and school visitations; demonstration lessons; action research; and collaborative lessons (Wepner et al., 2016).

Professional development should be self-directed and build on prior knowledge and experiences (Drago-Severson, 2004). It should help teachers to self-discover the urgency of appreciating the cultural and linguistic richness of their changing student population and learning the necessary instructional practices for teaching these students more effectively.

CONCLUSION

Administrators in suburban schools need to find ways to balance the many pressures that arise when once demographically similar communities change in color, culture, economic status, and linguistic orientation. They must first acknowledge the impact of these changes on their communities, teachers, staff, and students. They need to understand and appreciate how attitudes, perceptions, and beliefs influence teachers' and parents' responses to students and the schools (Evans, 2007).

With this awareness, they need to create conditions in their schools that contribute to diverse students' success (Tefera, Frankenberg, Siegel-Hawley, & Chirichigno, 2011) yet are ever-sensitive to White students' needs. Administrators are best served when they pursue a multifaceted organizational, programmatic, and professional development approach that subscribes to the unique needs of the schools' stakeholders.

REFLECTION QUESTIONS

1. What roles and responsibilities should school boards and local and statewide elected officials have in providing guidance and assistance to changing suburban school districts?
2. What do you think that school district and school-based administrators in changing suburban school districts can and should be able to do to close the achievement gap?
3. Which organizational structures, programs, and professional development opportunities would you use, and why, in a changing suburban school district?

REFERENCES

Bernstein, M. F. (2004, July 25). The urbanization of suburban classrooms. *New York Times,* pp. 1–2. Retrieved from http://www.nytimes.com

Burke, M. (2016, April 20). *A study of the preparedness of teachers of English language learners in Westchester County, New York.* Paper presented at the Seventh Annual Student Research Day, Manhattanville College, Purchase, NY.

Coalition of Community Schools. (2016). *What is a community school?* Retrieved from http://www.communityschools.org/aboutschools/what_is_a_community_school.aspx

Collier, V. P., & Thomas, W. P. (2009). *Education English learners for a transformed world.* Albuquerque, NM: Fuente Press.

Cook, L. (2015, January 15). U.S. education: Still separate and unequal. *U.S. News & World Report.* Retrieved from http://www.usnews.com/news/blogs/data-mine/2015/01/28/us-education-still-separate-and-unequal

Daresh, J. C., & Aplin, N. D. (2001). Educational leadership and the suburban superintendent. *Education, 107*(4), 209–218.

Darling-Hammond, L., & McLaughlin, M. W. (1995). Policies that support professional development in an era of reform. *Phi Delta Kappan, 76*(8), 597–604.

Diem, S., Frankenberg, E., Cleary, C., & Ali, N. (2014). The politics of maintaining diversity policies in demographically changing urban-suburban school districts. *American Journal of Education, 120*(3), 351–389. Retrieved from http://dx.doi.org/10.1086/675532

Drago-Severson, E. (2004). *Helping teachers learn. Principal leadership for adult growth and development.* Thousand Oaks, CA: Corwin.

Erwin, S., Winn, P., Gentry, J., & Cauble, M. (2010, April). *A comparison of urban, suburban, and rural principal leadership skills by campus student achievement level.* Proceedings of the annual Meeting of the American Educational Research Association SIG: Leadership for school improvement, Denver, CO.

Evans, A. E. (2007). Changing faces: Suburban school response to demographic change. *Education and Urban Society, 39*(3), 315–348. Retrieved from http://eus.sagepub.com/content/39/3/315

Fichter, M. (2012, October 3). Princeton plan for schools—good or bad? *Daily Edition.* Retrieved from http://2paragraphs.com/2012/10/princeton-plan-for-schools-good-or-bad

Gómez, D. W., Ferrara, J., Santiago, E., Fanelli, F., & Taylor, R. (2012). Full-service community schools: A district's commitment to educating the whole child. In A. Honigsfeld & A. Cohan (Eds.), *Breaking the mold of education for culturally and linguistically diverse students: Innovative and successful practices for the 21st century* (pp. 65–73). Lanham, MD: Rowman & Littlefield.

Hirsh, S. (2009). A new definition. *Journal of Staff Development, 30*(4), 10–16.

Holme, J. J., Diem, S., & Welton, A. (2013). Suburban school districts and demographic change: The technical, normative, and political dimensions of response. *Education Administration Quarterly 50*(1), 34-66. Retrieved from http://eaq.sagepub.com/content/50/1/34

Howard, G. (2007). As diversity grows, so must we. *Educational Leadership, 64*(6), 16–22.

Immigrate to Manitoba, Canada. (n.d.). *Immigration planning guide: Conduct an internal and external environmental scan.* Retrieved from http://www2.immigratemanitoba.com/browse/regionalcommunities/plan_guide/community-int_ext.html

Island Tree Schools. (n.d.). *Elementary reorganization.* Retrieved from islandtrees.org/PDFS/ELEMENARY_/REORG.PDF

Krashen, S. (2016). Why bilingual education? *National Association for Bilingual Education.* Retrieved from http://www.nabe.org/BilingualEducation

Ladson-Billings, G. (2006). From the achievement gap to the education debt: Understanding achievement in U.S. schools. *Educational Researcher, 35*(7), 3–12.

Magnet Schools of America. (n.d.). *What are magnet schools?* Retrieved from http://www.magnet.edu/about/what-are-magnet-schools

Moughamian, A. C., Rivera, M. O., & Francis, D. J. (2009). *Instructional models and strategies for teaching English languages learners.* Portsmouth, NH: RMC Research Corporation, Center on Instruction.

National Governors Association Center for Best Practices & Council of Chief State School Officers. (2010). *Common Core State Standards language arts.* Washington, DC: Author.

No Child Left Behind Act of 2001. (NCLB). Pub. L. No. 107-110, 115 Stat. 1425 (2002).

Nuzzo, J. (2013, December 4). SWR proceeds with Princeton Plan for elementary schools. *Riverhead News-Review.* Retrieved from http://riverheadnewsreview.timesreview.com/2013/12/49719/swr-proceeds-with-princeton-plan-for-elementary-schools

Pray, L. (2013). *Supporting English language learners in school and in afterschool and summers.* Retrieved from http://www.expandinglearning.org/sites/default/files/em_articles/1_supportingenglish.pdf

Ravitch, D. (2016, July 23). The common core costs billions and hurts students. *New York Times.* Retrieved from http://www.nytimes.com/2016/07/24/opinion/sunday/the-common-core-costs-billions-and-hurts-students.html

Santiago, E., Ferrara, J., & Quinn, J. (2012). *Whole child, whole school: Applying theory to practice in a community school.* Lanham, MD: Rowman & Littlefield.

Siegel-Hawley, G., & Frankenberg, E. (2011). Magnet school student outcomes: What the research says. *The National Coalition on School Diversity. Brief No. 6.* Retrieved from http://www.magnet.edu/files/policy-conference/diversityresearchbriefno6.pdf

Tefera, A., Frankenberg, E., Siegel-Hawley, G., & Chirichigno, G. (2011). *Integrating suburban schools: How to benefit from growing diversity and avoid segregation.* The Civil Rights Project/Proyecto Derechos Civiles, Los Angeles, CA. Retrieved from https://civilrightsproject.ucla.edu/research/k-12-education/integration-and-diversity/integrating-suburban-schools-how-to-benefit-from-growing-diversity-and-avoid-segregation

U.S. Department of Education. (2010). *Race to the top fund: Purpose.* Retrieved from http://www2.ed.gov/programs/racetothetop/index.html

Welton, A., Diem, S., & Holme, J. J. (2013). Color conscious, cultural blindness: Suburban school districts and demographic change. *Education and Urban Society, 47*(6), 695–722. Retrieved from http://eus.sagepub.com/content/47/6/695

Wepner, S. B., Ferrara, J., Rainville, K. N., Gómez, D. W., Lang, D. E., & Bigaouette, L. (2012). *Changing suburbs, changing students: Helping school leaders face the challenges.* Thousand Oaks, CA: Corwin.

Wepner, S. B., Gómez, D. W., Cunningham, K. E., Rainville, K. N., & Kelly, C. (2016). *Literacy leadership in changing schools: 10 keys to successful professional development.* New York, NY: Teachers College Press.

Wepner, S. B., & Hopkins, D. (Eds.) (2011). *Collaborative leadership in action: Partnering for success in schools.* New York, NY: Teachers College Press.

White Plains Public School District (n.d.). *Controlled parents' choice program.* Retrieved from http://www.Whiteplainspublicschools.org/Page/726

Wirt, G. (2013, August 27). MacCormack wants to preserve Montclair's magnet schools. *NorthJersey.com:News.* Retrieved from http://www.northjersey.com/news/maccormack-wants-to-preserve-montclair-s-magnet-schools-1.582683

Chapter Four

Lessons for Leaders about Educating English Learners

Douglas Fisher and Nancy Frey

- School leaders have a significant role in ensuring that English learners (ELs) access quality learning experiences.
- Significant amounts of relevant instructional time must be devoted to practicing language if ELs are going to progress in content and language learning.
- School leaders must be aware of discriminatory practices and track the progress of ELs to ensure the language assistance program is educationally sound.

As Bob Dylan so aptly noted, "The times, they are a-changin'." This is certainly the case in suburban schools when it comes to educating ELs. Historically, ELs were mostly educated in large urban school systems, often based in the city of their immigration. That is no longer the case, as nearly every district in the country—urban, suburban, and rural—now provides educational services for students learning English as an additional language (U.S. Department of Education, 2015).

Although immigration still accounts for a number of ELs, an increasing number of students learning English are born in the United States, and have attended American schools their entire lives. One of the most important things a school leader can remember about ELs is that they are not a monolithic group. There is much diversity in this population. ELs differ from native English speakers, and from one another, in a number of important ways, including:

- *Linguistic.* Spanish is the most common second language in the United States, but there are over a hundred different languages represented in many school districts. These languages differ in their pronunciation patterns and orthographic systems. Importantly, the more linguistically distant a student's primary language is from English, the greater the challenge in transferring his or her knowledge about language to English (e.g., Durgunoglu, 2002).
- *Home language proficiency.* Proficiency in a home or heritage language, especially one learned during infancy, facilitates learning in additional languages. The student's age and prior education greatly influence proficiency in his or her heritage language and thus impact transfer of knowledge to a new language. Some students are learning English with no formal heritage language knowledge, while others are leveraging what they formally know grammatically, syntactically, and semantically about their heritage language into English.
- *Number of languages spoken.* Some students enroll in schools having mastered more than one language. These students have significant linguistic flexibility that aids their acquisition of English. Others have spoken one language at home for years and their exposure to English is a new experience.
- *Poverty and trauma.* Living in poverty, facing food and/or housing insecurity, and experiencing trauma have a profound impact on the brain. When basic needs are not met, it is hard to focus on language learning.
- *Personality.* Differences in personality can lead to differences in language learning. Some students are outgoing and more social in nature, and they tend to learn languages more readily. Others are shy and quiet and may be less comfortable practicing their new language.

In many cases, the diversity of ELs is a source of pride as educators learn more about the heritage cultures of their students and work to build multilingual students who are prepared for a global economy. They celebrate the fact that they are contributing to a society in which individual differences are celebrated, and they seek out opportunities for English monolingual students to develop proficiency in other languages. In other cases, ELs are a source of stress and conflict.

Sadly, this is still the case more than forty years after the Supreme Court of the United States determined that in order for public schools to comply with their legal obligations under Title VI of the Civil Rights Act of 1964 (Title VI), they must take affirmative steps to ensure that ELs can meaningfully participate in appropriate educational programs and services.

In 2015, the U.S. Department of Justice and the U.S. Department of Education identified several areas that frequently result in noncompliance as school systems attempt to meet their federal obligations to ELs. According to the document, school systems, in partnership with their state education agency, must:

a. *Identify and assess EL students in need of language assistance in a timely, valid, and reliable manner;*
b. *Provide EL students with a language assistance program that is educationally sound and proven successful;*
c. *Sufficiently staff and support the language assistance programs for EL students;*
d. *Ensure EL students have equal opportunities to meaningfully participate in all curricular and extracurricular activities, including the core curriculum, graduation requirements, specialized and advanced courses and programs, sports, and clubs;*
e. *Avoid unnecessary segregation of EL students;*
f. *Ensure that EL students with disabilities under the Individuals with Disabilities Education Act (IDEA) or Section 504 are evaluated in a timely and appropriate manner for special education and disability-related services and that their language needs are considered in evaluations and delivery of services;*
g. *Meet the needs of EL students who opt out of language assistance programs;*
h. *Monitor and evaluate EL students in language assistance programs to ensure their progress with respect to acquiring English proficiency and grade level core content, exit EL students from language assistance programs when they are proficient in English, and monitor exited students to ensure they were not prematurely exited and that any academic deficits incurred in the language assistance program have been remedied;*
i. *Evaluate the effectiveness of a school district's language assistance program(s) to ensure that EL students in each program acquire English proficiency and that each program was reasonably calculated to allow EL students to attain parity of participation in the standard instructional program within a reasonable period of time;*
j. *Ensure meaningful communication with LEP parents.* (U.S. Department of Justice and U.S. Department of Education, 2015, pp. 9–10)

This list is particularly helpful to school leaders who want to do right by students and comply with federal laws and regulations.

This chapter focuses on actions that leaders can take to ensure that ELs thrive in their schools, beginning with identifying who ELs are. Hopefully, the district has policies and procedures in place to identify students learning English as an additional language so that services and supports can be organized and implemented. As noted in the *Dear Colleague Letter* (2015) from the U.S. Department of Justice and Department of Education:

> Most school districts use a home language survey (HLS) at the time of enroll-ment to gather information about a student's language background (e.g., first language learned, language the student uses most often, and languages used in the home). The HLS identifies those students who should be referred for an English language proficiency ("ELP") assessment to determine whether they should be classified as EL students, who are entitled to language assistance services. (p. 10)

The information gathered on the HLS should be used to make decisions about additional assessments that can be used to identify if a given student needs additional support to learn. From there, the role of the principal is to ensure that students access quality instruction. As Manna (2015) noted, prin-cipals are multipliers of effective teaching. ELs need, and deserve, effective teaching that ensures they can access the core curriculum offered by the school.

EFFECTIVE INSTRUCTION FOR ELS

In general, ELs benefit from the same quality instruction as any other stu-dent. Classrooms should have clear learning targets, and tasks and assign-ments should align with the learning targets. Teachers should regularly check for understanding, and teachers should respond when students do not learn what was expected. (For a more complete description of high-quality teach-ing, see Fisher, Frey, & Hite, 2016.)

ELs can be the canary in the coal mine, serving as early evidence that instruction is not working. If the lesson is not working for an EL, it is probably not working for most of the students in the classroom. Wise leaders notice the learning of their ELs, and use it as a proxy for determining the overall effectiveness of the classroom instruction. There are, however, some specific aspects of high-quality instruction that warrant more detail, given the role that they play in ensuring access for ELs.

Lesson Purpose

The first aspect relates to the lesson purpose. Nearly every teacher has an objective. Teachers generally know what they want students to learn. This is appropriate and well-documented in the research literature as valuable (e.g., Hattie, 2009).

ELs need more than teachers' objectives. They need teachers' learning expectations to have both content and language elements. Every lesson is an opportunity for students to learn content and language simultaneously. Consider the middle school physical education teacher who wants his students to understand the components of fitness. The class is engaged in playing soccer, and the learning target is: Students will understand the four main components of fitness as applied to soccer. The teacher also has several language-learning intentions for different days. Three of them are:

- Use technical vocabulary (*muscular strength, muscular endurance, flexibility*, and *cardiovascular endurance*) in their collaborative conversations.
- Use compare and contrast signal words—such as *more than, less than*—to summarize the main components of fitness.
- Describe how each fitness component is utilized in soccer, for example, "Muscle develops strength playing soccer," which grammatically requires the use of the present tense.

Each of these allows the physical education teacher to determine students' understanding and to make corrections during the lesson if students are not learning. Thus, the whole point of having a measurable objective has been met. But even more importantly, these language-related learning targets support ELs' development of their literacy skills. Additionally, they do no harm to students who are already proficient in English.

Notice that each of the three language intentions focuses on a different aspect of language learning. The first develops students' vocabulary, which is critically important for ELs. Learning a new language requires extensive word learning, and integrating vocabulary into lessons helps facilitate that knowledge acquisition. The second example provides students with an opportunity to work on language structure, specifically compare and contrast. The area of language structure also includes syntax, grammar, and formal use of language.

Often, teachers provide students with language frames so that they can be apprenticed into the structures of English, with the correct placement of verbs, for example. A group of elementary teachers developed the frames found in figure 4.1 to build their students' use of English language structures during social studies lessons.

The third example from the physical education class focuses on how learning the components of fitness centers on the functions of language. Humans use language for a variety of purposes, and teachers can help students, especially their ELs, match the function with the appropriate conventions. For example, language can be used to express an opinion, summarize, persuade, question, entertain, inform, sequence, disagree, debate, evaluate, or justify. Each of these functions has rules and conventions that ELs need to internalize.

Sample Language Frames

- I agree/disagree with _____ because _____.

- They say _____ and/but I say _____ because _____.

- Both _____ and _____ are alike/different because _____.

- After listening to _____ I found that _____.

- This event in history reminds me of _____ because _____. (making connection)

- This event happened because _____. (cause/effect)

- From the point of view of _____ ....

- Due to the fact that _____ (cause), _____ (effect) happened.

Figure 4.1.   Sample Language Frames

Relevance

A second aspect of learning intentions that is critical for ELs is relevance. Of course, learning should be relevant for all students, but ELs will strive to pay attention just that much longer if they understand why they are learning something. If you have never tried to learn or listen in another language, you have no idea how fatiguing it is to do so. When lessons are less relevant, students are at risk for tuning out because it is hard to pay attention in a new language for long periods of time.

Relevance is motivating and encourages students to push through the struggle and keep focused on the learning. Teachers should think through the *why* question when it comes to learning, not just the *what* question. That is to say that it is just as important for teachers to know why they are teaching as it is to know what they are teaching.

Consider the geometry teacher who tells her students that they need to know about triangles because this information is necessary for the test that they are having. Compare that with the geometry teacher who says, "We're analyzing exterior angles today because they are used in construction as well as in 2-D and 3-D graphic arts. Let's say you were checking that two lines were parallel, and if not the tabletop would slope down and the dishes would fall off. One way to check on this is to use the exterior angles of triangles. Let's see how in this next problem. Ready?" All students, and especially ELs, are more likely to persevere for the second teacher, even if the tasks assigned in the class are the same.

Relevance is an important point for leaders. Without relevance, the performance of students might be compromised, even by well-meaning teachers who use otherwise effective instructional approaches. Wise school leaders help their teachers set clear learning targets that include both content and language, recognizing that ELs are always doing the double work of learning the English language along with content. They also ensure that students know why they are learning the content they are being asked to learn.

When leaders visit classrooms, they should ask students:

- What are you learning today?
- Why are you learning that?
- How will you know if you've learned it?

The third question focuses on the success criteria that the teacher has established for all learners. Simply said, students should know what good and great work looks like, and be provided with examples of the quality that the teacher expects. This allows students to understand how their teacher will know if they have learned the content, which can provide them a window into their own understanding.

Classroom Talk

A third specific aspect of instruction that is critical for ELs is classroom talk. No one gets good at things that they do not do. The same is true for ELs. If they are not producing English, they are likely not learning English. Significant numbers of instructional minutes must be devoted to student-to-student interactions, in which students use academic language. There are a number of instructional routines that teachers can use to encourage students' talk. Some examples are found in figure 4.2.

Routine	Procedures	Focus on EL	Linguistic Frames
Barrier Games	One partner has a picture or information that the other partner does not have. Students sit back-to-back, or have a visual obstruction to block their view (barrier). Using oral language only, students communicate to complete the task. Tasks may require partners to draw a picture, place objects in specific positions, find the difference in 2 pictures, etc. Students in small groups might each have 1 picture in a sequence. Without looking at the other pictures, they must put them all in the correct order.	• Use for all levels of EL. • Use to practice survival vocabulary – food, body, clothing, school items, etc. • Use to reinforce concepts – pictures of the life cycle of a butterfly. • Use to practice language structures – prepositions, sequence words, etc. • Teach vocabulary students will need to complete the task.	• I see a _____. • Do you have a _____? • First you (draw, put, place,) ____. • I think _____ (my/your/her/his) picture goes _ (first, second, next, last), because ____. • There is a ___ (prepositional phrase – on top of, in between, etc.) the _____.
Busy Bees	Students mimic the buzzing sound and slow movement of bumblebees as they buzz around the room to find a partner. Teacher says "Busy bees, fly!" Students move around room and buzz until they hear, "Busy bees, land!" The "bee" they are standing next to becomes their partner for a brief learning activity such as giving an opinion or answering a question.	• Pair EL "bees" purposefully by giving them different colored cards – they must find a partner with another color. • Change the color each time you do it, so children cannot easily identify ELs. • Teach students expected behaviors such as looking at the person talking, turn taking. • Respect cultural norms regarding physical contact.	• My favorite ____ is _____. • What is your favorite ____? • I think that_____. • I think the funniest part was when _____. • I liked _____ the best because _____.

Figure 4.2.   Instructional Routines Useful for Building Academic Language

Explorers and Settlers	Assign half the students to be explorers and half to be settlers. Explorers seek out a settler to discuss a question. Repeat process 1-2 times to discuss the same question or a new, related question.	• Vary the assignment roles of explorer and settler so that ELs are not always one or the other. • Assign ELs at early levels of proficiency to be all explorers or settlers; then have the other group speak first to act as language models.	Sentence frames will vary depending on the prompt and the topic. Samples might include: • The best thing about __ is ___. • I still have a question about ___. • I'd like to know more about __. Can you tell me anything?
Find Someone Who… or Walking Review	Given a task to complete (i.e., a handout activity), students must find a classmate who can answer a question about the task. They ask the student the question, write down the response they are given and the name of the student who answered. This can be done as a review of learning, or in anticipation of learning. It can also be done in the form of BINGO.	• Require that the students write down the answer they hear to practice listening, writing, and speaking. • ELs at early levels of proficiency can have a differentiated handout of questions in familiar language that address the main idea.	• Do you know ___? • Have you found anyone who _? • Have you ever ___?
Numbered Heads Together	In groups of 4 or 5, each group is assigned a number. Each student within the group is assigned (or selects) a number one through four (or five if numbers necessitate). Teacher asks a question. Teacher tells students to make sure every student in the group can answer. After students have time to discuss, teacher spins overhead spinner and	• Provide structure and support so that ELs can respond to whole class questions. • Have students rehearse with their group what they will say to the class if EL's number is called upon to respond.	• I think you should say ___. • I think the answer is ___. • I'm not sure I know the answer. Is it ___?

Instructional Routines Useful for Building Academic Language

	announces the number of the student who must answer the question. Groups have one more minute to make sure that number student in their group knows the answer. The teacher spins again and announces the number of the group that must respond.		

Source: Adapted from Fisher, D., Frey, N., & Rothenberg, C. (2008). *Content area conversations: How to plan discussion-based lessons for diverse language learners.* Alexandria, VA: ASCD. Used with permission.

Instructional Routines Useful for Building Academic Language

Regardless of the specific strategy or routine used, the key is to devote sufficient time for students to practice the language(s) they are learning. School leaders and some researchers (e.g., Frey, Fisher, & Nelson, 2013) recommend approximately 50 percent of the instructional minutes, averaged across a week, be devoted to student-to-student interactions such that students are provided time to practice the language of the lesson. Leaders should engage teachers in conversations about the percentage of time they believe that students should be talking with one another.

Too often, schools do not have clear goals about student talk, and thus it is left to the discretion of individual teachers. In those cases, there is no cumulative effect on language learning because of the lack of attention to practice. Practice is not the only necessary element. The lack of practice has been a barrier for students learning English, not just in English. Leaders have to ensure that students have sufficient time to practice that which has been taught to them.

BEYOND HIGH-QUALITY INSTRUCTION

To avoid compliance issues related to ELs, school leaders must make clear that students are entitled to participate in the full range of offerings that the school has (Fisher & Frey, 2012). These offerings include sports, clubs, content-area classes, and so on. Too often, a well-meaning adult makes the case that a specific student would not benefit from a curricular or extracurricular experience.

Leaders have to listen carefully to the rationale and remember that even well-meaning adults may be discriminating against a student because of his or her current language proficiency. The law says that students have the *opportunity to meaningful participation*, which is an important distinction. That does not mean that they have to be forced into activities that they are not interested in, but it does mean that the school has to provide reasonable accommodations to ensure that students' participation is meaningful.

Consider the band director who wants to exclude a student because she does not speak fluent English, which makes it difficult to communicate with her. The exclusion would be considered discrimination. The school is responsible for ensuring that this student can participate meaningfully, which might include translations of instructions and peer support for staging. That is very different from a situation in which a student, who was provided language support for band tryouts, did not make the cut based on skill and performance.

In addition, school leaders have two other important responsibilities when it comes to ELs. First, they have to track the progress that students make in acquiring English proficiency and their mastery of grade-level core content. Wise administrators develop systems for progress monitoring ELs, and include interim language development assessments as well as teacher reports of content-area learning. Figure 4.3 contains a sample tool that can be used to track progress of ELs.

DEMOGRAPHICS

Student Name: _____ Grade: _____ School Year: _____

Date of Birth: _____ Gender: _____

Date of Entry to U.S. School: _____ Home Language: _____

Language Proficiency Level as of (date) _____

FAMILY COMMUNICATION NEEDS

Written communication preferences: _____

Telephone call preferences: _____

Face-to-face communication preferences: _____

School interpreter resource: _____

External Interpreter contact: _____

Staff advocate(s): _____

Peer advocate(s): _____

Home Visits	*Family Contacts*
Date:	Date:
Purpose:	Purpose:
Notes:	Notes:
Outcomes:	Outcomes:
Follow-up:	Follow-up:

ASPIRATIONS

What are the family's goals for their child? _____

_____

_____

What are the child's goals? _____

_____

_____

What needs to occur this year to forward these goals? _____

_____

ACADEMIC RECORDS

State academic performance exam results: ELA ____Math____ Science____ H/SS_____

College readiness tests: PSAT _____ SAT _____ ACT Subject Matter _____

Figure 4.3.   English Learner Tracking Form

Transcript analysis for graduation: _____

_____

NON-ACADEMIC INDICATORS

Health-related needs (dental, vision, hearing, physical, mental health, counseling):

_____

_____

_____

Extracurricular involvement:

Clubs _____ Afterschool enrollment _____ Sports _____

Student government _____ Tutoring _____

Other outside activities _____

Is student employed? _____

CURRENT SCHOOL YEAR PROGRESS MONITORING

Q1	Grades	Current GPA	EL Screening Results	Benchmark or Interim Assessment Results	Attendance
Q1					
Q2					
Q3					
Q4					

Class Schedule:

Teacher	Subject	Period

ENGLISH LANGUAGE LEARNER PROVISIONS

ELL Coordinator: _____

Service Provider(s) (include names, frequency, and duration of services):_____

_____

_____

English Learner Tracking Form

Although tracking progress is important, it is not sufficient to ensure that ELs benefit from the language-assistance program. When a teacher or leader notices that a student is not making progress, something has to change. School systems should not continue doing the same things that they did that were ineffective; they need to make changes to get better results. One of the roles of the leader is to monitor the progress of ELs and then facilitate changes with teachers and the instructional program to attain the desired results.

Finally, school leaders have to communicate with the families of the ELs they are fortunate to serve. The traditional ways of sending home a bilingual newsletter are not likely to be enough in today's society. Similarly, telling yourself that the auto-dialer message that was left for a family, even in the family's home language, was a job well done is problematic. Leaders should be using a wider range of tools to communicate with families and the broader community. For example, the app *Remind* allows for messages to be sent to all subscribers at once. Facebook, Twitter, and Instagram can be valuable methods for communicating events, successes, expectations, and such to families. Wise leaders work to brand their school as a welcoming place in which students are successful, and this requires effective and clear communication.

CONCLUSION

The demographics of suburban schools are changing. More often than not, suburban schools are educating ELs. But are they educating those students well and equitably? If not, a significant segment of the school population is at risk for failure in school, and perhaps in life. Who knows which student may develop new treatments for cancer, write the next great American novel, or lead his or her peers? We cannot afford to leave any student behind. Students need and deserve to have educational experiences that build their language and content knowledge. Although stated before, it bears repeating: Principals play a key role in ensuring that ELs receive the education that is mandated and that they need and deserve. Go forth and lead.

REFLECTION QUESTIONS

1. Nine areas have been identified by the U.S. Department of Justice and the U.S. Department of Education as essential for complying with federal law for ELs. In which of these areas is your school or district *not* compliant? What do you think needs to be done to ensure compliance?
2. Who is responsible for progress monitoring of students' acquisition of English? How often is this done? How is this communicated with families? What needs to change to ensure that students are acquiring English and that this information is communicated to families?

3. What types of assistance do the teachers in your school or district need to ensure that ELs have access to quality learning experiences?

REFERENCES

Durgunoglu, A. Y. (2002). Cross-linguistic transfer in literacy development and implications for language learners. *Annals of Dyslexia, 52*, 189–204.

Fisher, D., & Frey, N. (2012). *Essentials for principals: English language learners.* Bloomington, IN: Solution Tree.

Fisher, D., Frey, N., & Hite, S. A. (2016). *Intentional and targeted teaching: A framework for teacher growth and leadership.* Alexandria, VA: Association for Supervision and Curriculum Development.

Frey, N., Fisher, D., & Nelson, J. (2013). It's all about the talk. *Kappan, 94*(6), 8–13.

Hattie, J. (2009). *Visible learning: A synthesis of over 800 meta-analyses relating to achievement.* New York, NY: Routledge.

Manna, P. (2015). *Developing excellent school principals to advance teaching and learning: Considerations for state policy.* New York, NY: The Wallace Foundation.

Remind. (2011). [Mobile application software]. Available at https://www.remind.com/

U.S. Department of Education. (2015). *Digest of education statistics, 2014.* Retrieved from https://nces.ed.gov/programs/digest/2015menu_tables.asp

U.S. Department of Justice and U.S. Department of Education. (2015, January 7). *Dear colleague letter.* Retrieved from www2.ed.gov/about/offices/list/ocr/letters/colleague-el-201501.pdf

Chapter Five

A Conceptual Framework for the Educational Success of Dual Language Learners

Reducing the Achievement Gap

Eugene E. García

- Dual language learners' (DLLs) social and economic characteristics affect academic performance.
- Four critical elements—family, education, community, and brain development—need to be considered in understanding DLLs' academic achievement.
- A more integrative educational framework needs to be considered for DLLs.

Cross-culturally, children acquire the language of their respective speech communities, and do so effortlessly and without instruction (Pinker, 2007). Despite the great complexity of language, children already know most of its intricacies by age five. The most active acquisition period is in the preschool years. Children learn an average of ten new words per day, often with only one exposure to the word and in highly ambiguous circumstances (Spiegel & Halberda, 2011).

Languages differ across communities of speakers, and across individuals as well. Speech communities have considerable internal variation, even to the level of individual speakers (*idiolects*), and speakers may be members of multiple speech communities. Thus, a particular language is a set of expressions defined by a grammar, a psychological mechanism that maps sound to meaning in the mind/brain of a speaker-listener, and a vocabulary.

However, a child's tacit understanding of language use is also sensitive to social and situational contexts. The interpretation of particular linguistic expressions is tied to a language user's appreciation of relevance, coherence, and context (Gee, 2004). Literacy and other school subjects make use of a child's language ability, but they are substantially different in character. Humans acquire language by instinct, the way birds acquire birdsong, but the learning of school subjects, such as literacy, physics, and mathematics, does not follow a biologically endowed program.

While all typically developing children learn a vocabulary and a grammatical system, not all children will come to know specific facts about history or mathematics. Similarly, developing school language reflects the acquisition of language specific to a particular human context—namely, the world of formal schooling.

This chapter provides a comprehensive conceptual framework to assist in addressing the needs of multilingual learners in various heterogeneous learning contexts, particularly useful in suburban environments. The conceptual framework identifies an important constellation of elements that must be considered in providing educational practices that enable multilingual students to attain educational success. The framework serves as a way to think about what it takes to ensure positive educational outcomes in light of the existing achievement gap.

DUAL LANGUAGE AND MULTIPLE LANGUAGE DEVELOPMENT IN SUBURBAN SCHOOLS

It is common for young children and young adults around the world to be placed in circumstances in which they are acquiring more than one language in the home and in formal education settings (Castro, 2014; United Nations, 2009). In the United States, this population of children and students includes both long-term natives as well as recent immigrants to the country (Hernandez, Denton, & Mccartney 2011). Significant research, policy, and practice have given attention to the multilingual student population at various levels of schooling (August & Hakuta, 1997; August & Shanahan, 2006; California Department of Education, 2010; Office of English Language Acquisition, Language Enhancement, and Academic Achievement for Limited English Proficient Students, 2013).

The U.S. Department of Education has endorsed the use of DLL as a term that acknowledges the linguistic assets of U.S. children who are in circumstances in which multiple languages are part of their linguistic environment inside and outside of school settings (National Center for English Language Acquisition, 2015). However, many states, continue to use the terms limited English proficient (LEP) or English language learner (ELL).

These terms can be perceived as using a deficit-based perspective, and do not recognize that children engaged in learning more than one language have a greater likelihood of being bilingual, an attribute that can support executive function and other cognitive advantages (Bialystok, 2010). The term DLL is used in this chapter to dismiss any myth that multilingualism is a deficit. Multilingualism is an advantage.

Demographic trends indicate that DLLs are rapidly becoming the majority population of children distributed across urban, suburban, and rural communities. By 2020, DLLs are projected to become 50 percent of the population of children under the age of five (Frey, 2015).

The representation of DLLs in U.S. schools has its highest concentration in early education. The percentage of DLL students from pre-kindergarten to grade 5 rose from 4.7 to 7.4 from 1980 to 2012. Young DLLs (ages 0–8 years) have been the fastest-growing student population in the country over the past few decades, primarily a result of new immigration into the United States over the last two decades (Hernandez, Denton, & Mccartney, 2011).

Schools remain at the forefront of immigrant youth's integration into U.S. society, and some schools are clearly more prepared to assist the educational success of DLLs than others. The majority of new immigrants in the Midwest perceived that the elementary schools were doing a good job teaching DLLs. New immigrants in southern communities had less favorable perceptions of the elementary schools (Griffith, 2008).

Current Status of Educating DLLs

Currently, in U.S. schools, DLL students lag behind their monolingual same-age/grade peers at all proficiency levels of reading and mathematics by at least one-half of a standard deviation, starting at kindergarten and continuing through grade 12 (Garcia & Náñez, 2011). However, to adequately understand the academic performance patterns of DLL students as a whole, their social and economic characteristics must be considered and compared with native English speakers and the institutional history of U.S. schools (Garcia & Garcia, 2012).

While a great deal of socioeconomic variation exists among DLLs, they are more likely than native English-speaking children, on average, to live in poverty and have parents with limited formal education. In addition, DLL students are more likely to be an ethnic/racial minority (Hernandez, Denton, & Mccartney, 2011). Each of these factors—low income, low parent education, and ethnic/racial minority status—decreases group achievement averages across academic areas, leading to the relatively low performance of DLL students (Garcia & Náñez, 2011).

Thus, rather than pointing to one or two student background factors that account for the low achievement of DLL students, it should be understood that educational risk, in general, is attributable to a myriad of interrelated out-of-school factors, including parent education levels, family income, parent English language proficiency, mother's marital status at the time of birth, and single- versus dual-parent homes. While the education of these children and students in the United States is a continuous story of inequities and unrealized potentials (Gándara & Hopkins, 2010; Garcia & Frede, 2010), it need not be in the future, especially in changing suburban schools.

For the DLL population of children and students, there is a growing body of evidence indicating that young children can attain proficiency in more than one language without difficulty (Bialystok, 2010; New America Foundation, 2015). Instructional arrangements and strategies targeting these children specifically can produce positive developmental and learning outcomes (Calderon, 2010; California Department of Education, 2010; Genesee, Lindholm-Leary, Saunders, & Christian, 2006; Wright, 2015).

Misunderstandings and stereotypes about DLLs and their subgroups abound, partly because the processes of development and learning when acquiring two or more languages are quite complex. A single frame of reference cannot be used to judge their development. Linguistic properties between language systems and language processing influence one another as DLLs navigate many diverse social and academic environments. These environments must be taken into account when making professional and educational decisions about DLLs.

Currently, contributions to the education of DLLs have focused on differences between the DLL and non-DLL populations, but little attention has been paid to the heterogeneity *within* the DLL population or DLLs' trajectories across various developmental domains. Studies on the development of DLLs have focused primarily on institutional learning and developmental contexts with attention to linguistic factors rather than other developmental and contextual influences (Garcia & Markos, 2015).

Federal, state, and district policies are part of the sociopolitical and historical contexts affecting DLLs' experiences in educational settings. Additionally, the absence of shared and clear concepts and definitions, as well as the use of teaching methodologies not specific to the DLL population, make it difficult to interpret and explain educational interventions.

Proposed Changes to Educating ELLs

In light of this state of affairs, learning and teaching must be grounded in a conceptual framework that has a better understanding of DLL development and recognizes language development as interdependent with and situated in cultural practices and specific institutions. A conceptual framework for teaching DLLs must consider individual student attributes, including a new understanding of biological and neurological factors. Such a framework should acknowledge the ideal and material dimensions of culture (Bornstein & Cheah, 2006; Cole, 1996; Rogoff, 2013) and view culture as patterned, dynamic, historically grounded, and instrumental in students' learning (Artiles, 2003).

Culture affords and constrains human behavior, including language. Language and human development are cultural phenomena constituted by the interlocking of individual, interpersonal, and institutional dimensions (Rogoff, 2003). An individual acts to engage and develop culture in everyday activities within ecological niches in which the individual and her or his language play a key role (Weisner, 2005).

This is an important departure from traditional child and language development frameworks, for it transcends the exclusive analytic foci primarily on individual language traits and factors of language only. The proposed conceptual framework acknowledges that language must be examined and understood in the context of everyday practices in which interpersonal/sociocultural processes play a significant mediating role. Moreover, just as individuals use their linguistic skills and capacities in interpersonal contexts, it also acknowledges that individuals participate in social practices that are always located in institutional milieus.

The institutional layer is constituted by rules, expectations, and roles that can be invisible to observers. For instance, vocabulary expectations or participation in adult language practices are shaped, in part, by institutional assumptions and historical expectations in the communities in which individuals participate. A traditional conceptual framework is concerned with patterns of development over time, but the developmental trajectories (or pathways) also must document and account for variability within patterns.

That is, a framework should be mindful of patterned changes throughout the lifespan, as well as heterogeneity within and across developmental patterns. In addition, the student's participation in everyday activities is a central analytic focus of this proposed framework that calls for situated analyses of language development. The framework also takes into consideration the role of biological and neurological factors linked to development, learning, and language development (Goldman & Pellegrino, 2015).

The general plasticity of the brain through critical periods of language development and related epistemological effects specific to the DLL experiences is an important set of emerging empirical relationships that informs this proposed conceptual framework. For example, a group of DLLs between the ages of six and ten were asked to listen to speech sounds in English while being scanned with functional Magnetic Resonance Imaging (Garcia & Náñez, 2011). DLLs between the ages of eight and ten showed a very different pattern of activity, with increased brain activity in the areas of motor planning (inferior frontal gyrus), executive function (middle frontal gyrus), and attention (superior and inferior parietal cortices). The different patterns of brain activity for DLLs can affect how they learn a second language.

CONCEPTUAL FRAMEWORK'S CONSTELLATION OF ELEMENTS

The proposed conceptual framework builds on significant contributions by the National Research Council on the development and learning of DLLs (Allen & Kelly, 2015; August & Hakuta, 1997; Bowerman, Donovan, & Burns, 2000; Bransford, Brown, & Cocking, 1999; Shonkoff & Phillips, 2000; Snow & Van Hemel, 2008). The framework is founded on sociocultural and historical perspectives (Garcia & Garcia, 2012; Rogoff, 2003). As such, it emphasizes that an individual's development cannot be understood isolated from the social, cultural, and historical contexts in which it occurs.

The framework moves educational interventions away from assumptions and expectations about developmental competencies rooted in monolingual, cognitive perspectives and mainstream cultural practices. Most importantly, it challenges the notion that differences in development between DLLs and their monolingual peers equate to deficiencies (Cole & Cole, 2010; Genesee, 2010). This framework includes a constellation of interrelated elements that may facilitate or impede DLLs' optimal development.

It incorporates individual child characteristics, early child care and rearing, early learning, and K–12 educational experiences. It considers family, community, and social characteristics, and includes individual psychological and neurological circumstances as important elements in the DLL's learning experiences.

Family Circumstances

As with all children, the family serves as the most salient and enduring context in which DLLs learn and develop. Understanding the demographic profile is an initial step in understanding what DLL families "look like," but is not enough for uncovering the rich processes that both characterize and distinguish the context of DLL families. Processes related to culture-specific parenting and literacy practices related to bilingualism serve as key aspects of the family that are unique to DLLs.

While family demographics, such as social economic status, are often relied on to discuss family influences on development, overreliance on demographic characteristics may be insufficient for describing how family features influence development. One example is how DLLs are more likely to live in homes with grandparents, other relatives, or nonrelatives than their monolingual, English-speaking peers. While such living environments may initially be viewed as overcrowded and therefore a possible detriment to development, upon further investigation, the more people living in the home may be found to provide DLLs with additional learning opportunities for enriched language and other cultural experiences (Garcia & Garcia, 2012).

The recurrent, highly emotional theme present in discussions with DLLs' parents is the fear that the families' home language will be lost to the children when confronted with English-only formal education, thus minimizing critical supportive interaction between students and their limited-English-speaking family members. Other features of the family context should be considered, such as culture-specific parenting practices, beliefs, and goals, as well as the language and literacy practices promoted in the home in both the heritage language and English.

Formal Care and Educational Circumstances

A premise of this conceptual framework is that developmental and learning capacities are the result of the interaction between what children bring into the "educational" situation and what is being offered to them in that setting. Moreover, it acknowledges that formal "schooling" is critical for academic achievement and the general well-being of DLLs. However, in formal care and educational settings, it is important to understand what is being offered to DLLs, how it interacts with characteristics of the child (e.g., proficiency levels of native language [L1] and second language [L2], social-emotional strengths, and background knowledge), and how these learning opportunities are related to developmental capacities and future academic achievement.

The features of successful academic programs serving DLLs from pre-K to grade 12 highlight the need for well-qualified DLL teachers who receive extensive professional development. Other characteristics of successful programs are adequate teacher-student ratios, responsive and enriched language interactions, individualized adult-child conversations that promote language and positive relationships, opportunities for children to learn and practice new vocabulary and complex literacy, frequent assessment, and parent engagement (Genesee, Lindholm-Leary, Saunders, & Christian, 2006).

The specific needs of students vary as a result of ethnic origin and cultural attributes associated with ethnicity and individual learning capacities. Asian students, for example, vary in their academic success in English based on family and community structures that are available to support students. Not all "Asians" generate positive academic achievement profiles (Asian American Legal Defense Fund, 2008). And DLL students with special needs require special instructional attention, but do not seem to be at any risk by exposure to multiple languages (Artiles & Klingner, 2006).

The language of instruction has been the most intensely debated aspect of the education policy and practice for DLLs in pre-K–12 settings for decades, and is often politically charged (Gándara & Hopkins, 2010). In general, educators and researchers agree that to succeed in U.S. schools and participate in civic life in the United States, all children need to develop strong English proficiency and literacy skills.

The debate surrounds the question of how to best support the acquisition of English and whether it should come at the expense of decreased attention to the development and maintenance of the child's home language (L1). Questions about the ongoing role of L1 as English skills deepen have not been resolved. What is the role of L1? What is the social and cultural cost of losing proficiency in the home language? What is the role of education programs in systematically supporting L1, and what are the community values that may promote English-only approaches?

Enrollment in high-quality pre-kindergarten programs boosts the English language scores of Hispanic/Latino DLLs (Hammer, Davison, Lawrence, & Miccio, 2009). When preschool programs systematically expose DLLs to English within the context of a high-quality program, their English proficiency scores at kindergarten entry improve. Furthermore, there is a convergence of evidence that supporting a student's home language while adding English promotes higher levels of achievement in English (Castro, Páez, Dickinson, & Frede, 2011).

At best, instruction that systematically includes L1 contributes to growth in both English and home language skills; at worst, there is no difference in English language skills, but an advantage in home language growth (Barnett, Yarosz, Thomas, Jung, & Blanco, 2007; Durán, Roseth, & Hoffman, 2010; Farver, Lonigan, & Eppe, 2009). Effective curricula and instructional practices appear to be beneficial for both monolingual English speakers and DLLs (Slavin & Cheung, 2005).

The value of effective teaching on the learning experiences of DLLs has been well documented. Reading comprehension is an area of struggle for DLLs. Explaining vocabulary words and using them in different contexts (Collins, 2010) as well as strengthening oral language skills (Lesaux, 2009) have improved reading comprehension. Moreover, knowledge of academic language, the development of narrative and listening-comprehension skills, and an understanding of complex grammatical structures are all important for reading achievement in English (University of Chicago, 2010).

To be effective educators of DLLs, teachers need to be knowledgeable in five major content areas: (1) language development (e.g., syntax, phonology) of both the first and the second language; (2) the role of culture and its linkage to language development; (3) effective instructional practices to promote development and learning in DLLs; (4) the role of assessment and assessment strategies with DLLs; and (5) the teacher's role as a professional in the education of DLLs (National Association for the Education of Young Children, 1996).

Lastly, strong school–family partnerships are the hallmark of high-quality early education. Parent education, family visitation, parent conferences, and home–school communication interventions with DLL populations are "promising" strategies (Mathematica Policy Research, 2010). Sending literacy materials home in the family's primary language and sharing strategies to conduct literacy activities can increase the frequency of home literacy activities and promote literacy skill development in DLLs (Hancock, 2002).

Through partnerships with families, teachers can engage in dialogues to learn about families' childrearing beliefs and practices, as well as their expectations for their children's development and learning (Delgado-Gaitan, 2004).

Community and Societal Circumstances

The societal context and its community features impact DLLs' daily experiences. For example, one community feature highlighted in the conceptual model is the presence and value of different languages in a community where the people come together and interact. It is within these community spaces that DLLs and their families have more or fewer opportunities to hear different languages, interact with speakers of different languages, observe everyday and academic uses of language and literacy, and value their heritage languages and bilingualism.

Opportunities for diverse and frequent linguistic interactions increase the likelihood that DLLs will become bilingual. In contrast, limited opportunities to use a language within their community can hinder a DLL's development in that language. Along with language use, values related to bilingualism and multiculturalism and feelings of acceptance are important features in the community context.

The development and learning of language for DLLs must include attention to social and educational policies as well as the immigration and integration history of their families. Social policies, such as anti-immigrant rules, may disrupt family unification, have detrimental effects on DLL development, and negatively shape the way children form their psychological and social identities (Bean, Brown, & Bachmeier, 2015).

In academic learning settings, immigrant and refugee DLL children may have their learning experiences narrowed as a result of teachers' negative perceptions regarding their capacities to learn in English. This is a direct form of discrimination that most English-speaking children do not experience (Migration Policy Institute, 2015).

Also within the societal context, the extent to which the DLL's family has integrated into mainstream society, whether the DLL is a child of an immigrant or native-born parent, impacts DLLs' development and learning. For Native American children, the development of the heritage language is key for community participation and self-identity development, which is of critical importance for the family. English development, though, can enhance their academic learning (McCarty & Nicholas, 2014).

DLLs and the Brain

The significance for understanding the linguistic, social, and cultural circumstances of DLLs is clear. Recent evidence indicates that these circumstances also influence specific development of neural connectivity, plasticity, and cognitive control in the brain. The learning of two languages does not occur within an entirely static neurological system. The brain is affected by a person's environment, as it constrains the information taken in by a particular individual. This "dance" between the brain and the environment leads to the need to develop more dynamic models of development.

Hernandez, Dapretto, Mazziotta, and Bookheimer (2001) have proposed a new dynamic model of bilingualism that builds on general connectionist (i.e., neural network) models of language development as well as models of bilingualism (Abutalebi & Green, 2008). These models of bilingualism have identified three separate factors that contribute to understanding brain activity of bilingualism: age of acquisition, language proficiency, and cognitive control.

Whereas each of these factors has been considered independently, few have considered how these three factors might interact in time. For example, less proficient bilinguals show more brain activity in areas devoted to cognitive control (Gigi, Green, Abutalebi, & Grady, 2011). This acknowledged link between brain development and DLLs has only just begun to surface, but is beginning to expose attributes of DLLs' variations in language ability (Abutalbei & Green, 2008; Bialystok, 2010).

IMPLICATIONS OF THE CONCEPTUAL FRAMEWORK

This proposed conceptual framework draws from extant and emerging developmental frameworks related to DLLs with the purpose to motivate and inform research, policy, and practice for DLLs in the United States. The conceptual framework recognizes that family and community are increasingly characterized by linguistic and cultural diversity as global forces shape the world. Such diversity brings with it challenges and opportunities.

Challenges come from the complex interrelationships of diverse languages, cultures, and sociocultural practices that work in concert with individual psychological, neurological, and biological mechanisms. All the elements act interchangeably to influence the development of DLLs. The question becomes, how do educators use this knowledge of complexity for the benefit of students?

At present, a deep understanding of this complexity is obscured by frameworks that focus on development from simplistic monolingual perspectives.

At the same time, linguistic and cultural diversity affords opportunities for individual DLLs, their families, their communities, and indeed the nation as the world becomes increasingly globalized.

Language, culture, and their accompanying values are acquired in home and community environments. Children come to early care and early learning environments with some knowledge about what language is, how it works, and for what it is used. Children learn higher-level cognitive and communicative skills as they engage in socially meaningful activities. Children's development and learning are best understood as the interaction of linguistic, sociocultural, and cognitive knowledge and experiences.

Current approaches to research, policy, and practice concerning DLLs tend to adopt a monolingual approach providing a very limited understanding of bilingual and multilingual learners. A more appropriate approach is one that recognizes that development and learning are embedded in environments that are often unique to DLLs and that these features are taken into account in the conceptualization, design, implementation, and analysis of their early care and formal education, pre-K–12.

This conceptual framework asserts that:

- the development and learning of multiple languages in DLLs are critically important in understanding the development, learning, and well-being of DLLs;
- dual language learning is an inherently socially embedded process intersecting with neurological and biological determinants of development and learning;
- the acquisition of two languages in young children has no inherent negative social, linguistic, cognitive, or educational consequences and, to the contrary, may generate advantages in specific social, linguistic, cognitive, and academic domains;
- understanding development and learning of DLLs requires understanding the array of activities that are practiced by children in and outside of formal care and learning venues in families, communities, and societies in which they reside;
- ways in which children participate in day-to-day activities should inform the design and implementation of early care and formal learning opportunities/environments, pre-K–12;
- educational institutions and their policies and practices play a critical role in the development and learning of DLLs with an emerging consensus that achievement outcomes can be significantly improved; and
- linguistic and cultural diversity can afford opportunities for individual DLLs, their families, their communities, and indeed the nation as the world becomes increasingly globalized.

CONCLUSION

Students' language development reflects their sociocultural circumstances and bioneurological characteristics. DLLs, in particular, experience a host of factors in and out of school that affect their ability to learn English. It is incumbent upon educational institutions to be mindful of these factors when developing academic programs focused on both language acquisition and content-area learning. Programs that are integrative, comprehensive, and functional will advance the circumstances of DLLs, particularly those now living in suburban contexts.

REFLECTION QUESTIONS

1. Why does language development need to be examined and understood in the context of everyday practices?
2. What does it mean to be an effective educator of DLLs?
3. Summarize your understanding of the conceptual framework proposed in this chapter and, in your summary, highlight two key concepts that should be shared with other educators.

REFERENCES

Abutalebi, J., & Green, D. W. (2008) Control mechanisms in bilingual language production: Neural evidence from language switching studies. *Language and Cognitive Processes, 23*, 557–582.

Allen, L., & Kelly, B. B. (2015). *Professional learning for the early care and education workforce*. Washington, DC: National Research Council.

Artiles, A. (2003). "Special education's changing identity: Paradoxes and dilemmas in views of culture and space." *Harvard Educational Review*, 73(2). 164–202.

Artiles, A. & Klinger, J.K. (2006). "Forging a knowledge base on English language learners with special needs: Theoretical population and technical issues." *Teachers College Record, 108*(11), 1–7.

Asian American Legal Defense Fund. (2008). Retrieved from immigrationtounitedstates.org/357-asian-amreican-legal-defense-fund.html.

August, D., & Hakuta, K. (1997). *Improving schooling for language-minority children: A research agenda*. Washington, DC: National Research Council, Institute of Medicine, National Academy Press.

August, D., & Shanahan, T. (Eds.) (2006). *Developing literacy in second language learners: Report of the national literacy panel on language minority youth and children*. Mahwah, NJ: Lawrence Erlbaum Associates.

Barnett, W. S., Yarosz, D. J., Thomas, J., Jung, K., & Blanco, D. (2007). *Two-way and monolingual English immersion in preschool education: An experimental comparison*. New Brunswick, NJ: National Institute for Early Education Research.

Bean, F. D., Brown, S. K., & Bachmeier, J. (2015). *Parents without papers: The progress and pitfalls of Mexican American integration*. New York, NY: Russell Sage Foundation.

Bialystok, E. (2010). Global-local and trail-making tasks by monolingual and bilingual children: Beyond inhibition. *Developmental Psychology, 46*(1), 93–105.

Bornstein, M. H., & Cheah, C. S. L. (2006). The place of "culture and parenting" in the ecological contextual perspective on developmental science. In K. H. Rubin and O. B. Chung (Eds.), *Parenting beliefs, behaviors, and parent-child relations. A cross-cultural perspective* (pp. 3–34). New York, NY: Psychology Press.

Bowerman, B. T., Donovan, S. M., & Burns, M. S. (2000). *Eager to learn: Educating our preschoolers.* Washington, DC: National Research Council.

Bransford, J. D., Brown, A., & Cocking, R. R. (1999). *How people learn.* Washington, DC: National Research Council.

Calderón, M. E. (2010). *Teaching reading & comprehension to English learners, K–5.* New York, NY: Solution Tree.

California Department of Education. (2010). *Improving education for English learners: Research-based approaches.* Sacramento, CA: Author.

Castro, D. (2014). The development of early care and education of dual language learners: Examining the state of the knowledge. *Early Childhood Research Quarterly, 29,* 693–698.

Castro, D. C., Páez, M. M., Dickinson, D. K., & Frede, E. (2011). Promoting language and literacy in young dual language learners: Research, practice, and policy. *Child Development Perspectives, 5*(1), 15–21.

Cole, M. (1996). *Cultural psychology: A once and future discipline.* Cambridge, MA: Belkap Press.

Cole, M., & Cole, S. R. (2010). *The development of children.* New York, NY: Worth.

Collins, M. F. (2010). ELL preschoolers' English vocabulary acquisition from storybook reading. *Early Childhood Research Quarterly, 25*(1), 84–97.

Delgado-Gaitan, C. (2004). *Involving Latino families in schools: Raising student achievement through home-school partnerships.* Thousand Oaks, CA: Corwin Press.

Durán, L., Roseth, C., & Hoffman, P. (2010). An experimental study comparing English-only and transitional bilingual education on Spanish-speaking preschoolers' early literacy development. *Early Childhood Research Quarterly, 25*(2), 207–217.

Farver, J. M., Lonigan, C. J., & Eppe, S. (2009). Effective early literacy skill development for young Spanish-speaking English language learners: An experimental study of two methods. *Child Development, 80*(3), 703–719.

Frey, W. H. (2015). *Diversity explosion: How new racial demographics are remaking America.* Washington, DC: The Brookings Institution.

Gándara, P., & Hopkins, M. (2010). *Forbidden languages: English learners and restrictive language policies.* New York, NY: Teachers College Press.

Garcia, E. E., & Frede, E. C. (Eds.) (2010). *Young English language learners.* New York, NY: Teachers College Press.

Garcia, E. E., & Garcia, E. H. (2012). *Understanding the language development and early education of hispanic children.* New York, NY: Teachers College Press.

Garcia, E., & Markos, A. (2015). Early childhood education and dual language learners. In W. E. Wright, S. Boun, & O. Garcia (Eds.), *The handbook of bilingual and multilingual education* (pp. 146–171). Malden, MA: John Wiley & Sons.

Garcia, E., & Náñez, J. (2011). *Bilingualism and cognition: Joining cognitive psychology and education to enhance bilingual research, pedagogy and policy.* Washington, DC: American Psychological Association.

Gee, J. P. (2004). *Situated language and learning: A critique of traditional schooling.* New York, NY: Taylor and Francis.

Genesee, F. (2010). Dual language development in preschool children. In E. E. Garcia & E. C. Frede (Eds.), *Young English language learners* (pp. 59–79). New York, NY: Teachers College Press.

Genesee, F., Lindholm-Leary, K., Saunders, B., & Christian, D. (2006). *Educating English language learners: A synthesis of research evidence.* New York, NY: Cambridge University Press.

Gigi, L., Green, D. W., Abutalebi, J., & Grady, C. (2011). Cognitive control for language switching in bilinguals. *Language and Cognitive Processes, 27,* 1479–1488.

Goldman, S., & Pellegrino, J. W. (2015). Research on learning and instruction: Implications for curriculum, instruction and assessment. *Behavioral and Brain Sciences, 2*(1), 33–41.

Griffith, D. (2008). New midwesterners, new southerners: Immigration experiences in four rural American settings. In D. S. Massey (Ed.), *New faces in new places: The changing geography of American immigration* (pp. 179–210). New York, NY: Russell Sage Foundation.

Hammer, C. S., Davison, M. D., Lawrence, F. R., & Miccio, A. W. (2009). The effect of maternal language on bilingual children's vocabulary and emergent literacy development during head start and kindergarten. *Scientific Studies of Reading, 13*(2), 99–121.

Hancock, D. R. (2002). The effects of native language books on the pre-literacy skill development of language minority kindergartners. *Journal of Research in Childhood Education, 17*(1), 62–68.

Hernandez, A. E., Dapretto, M., Mazziotta, J., & Bookheimer, S. (2001). Language switching and language representation in Spanish-English bilinguals: An MRI study. *NeuroImage, 14*, 510–520.

Hernandez, D. J., Denton, N. A., & Mccartney, S. E. (2011). Early childhood education programs: Accounting for low enrollment in newcomer and native families. In R. Alba & M. Waters (Eds.), *The next generation: Immigrant youth and families in a comparative perspective* (pp. 46–68). New York, NY: New York University Press.

Lesaux, N. (2009, October). *Vocabulary and academic language.* Slide presentation at the Hewlett Foundation Workshop on the Role of Language in School Learning: Implications for Closing the Achievement Gap, Menlo Park, CA.

Mathematica Policy Research. (2010). *Identifying enhanced instructional practices that support English language learners: Background literature review.* Washington, DC: Author.

McCarty, T. L., & Nicholas, S. E. (2014). Reclaiming indigenous languages: A reconsideration of roles and responsibilities of schools. In K. M. Borman, T. G. Wiley, D. R. Garcia, & A. B. Danzig (Eds.), *Review of Research in Education, vol. 38* (pp. 106–136). Washington, DC: American Educational Research Association.

Migration Policy Institute. (2015). *The impact of discrimination on the early schooling experiences of children of immigrant families.* Washington, DC: Author

National Association for the Education of Young Children. (1996). *NAEYC position paper: Responding to linguistic and cultural diversity—Recommendations for effective early childhood education.* Washington, DC: Author.

National Center for English Language Acquisition. (2015). *English learner tool kit for state and local education authorities (SEA and LEA).* Washington, DC: Author. Retrieved from http://www2.ed.gov/about/offices/list/oela/english-learner-toolkit/eltoolkit.pdf

New America Foundation. (2015). *Boomtown kids: Harnessing energy and aligning resources for dual language learners in San Antonio, Texas.* Washington, DC: Author.

Office of English Language Acquisition, Language Enhancement, and Academic Achievement for Limited English Proficient Students. (2013). *The biennial report to Congress on the implementation of the title III state formula grant program, school years 2008–10.* Washington, DC: Author. Retrieved from http://www.ncela.us/files/uploads/3/Biennial_Report_0810.pdf

Pinker, S. (2007). *The stuff of thought: Language as a window into human nature.* New York, NY: Viking.

Rogoff, B. (2003). *The cultural nature of human development.* New York, NY: Oxford University Press.

Rogoff, B. (2013). *Developing destinies: A Mayan midwife and town.* London, UK: Oxford University Press.

Shonkoff, J., & Phillips, D. (2000). *From neurons to neighborhoods: The science of early childhood development.* Washington, DC: National Research Council.

Slavin, R. E., & Cheung, A. (2005). A synthesis of research on language of reading instruction for English language learners. *Review of Education Research, 75*(2), 247–284.

Snow, C. E., & Van Hemel, S. B. (Eds.) (2008). *Early childhood assessment: Why, what, and how.* Washington, DC: The National Academies Press.

Spiegel, C., & Halberda, J. (2011). Rapid fast-mapping abilities in 2-year-olds. *Journal of Experimental Child Psychology, 109*(1), 132–140.

United Nations. (2009). *International migrant stock: The 2008 revision (POP/DB/MIG/ Rev.2005)*. [Data file] Retrieved from http://esa.un.org/migration.

University of Chicago. (2010). *Getting on track early for school success: An assessment system to support effective instruction*. Chicago, IL: Author.

Weisner, T. S. (2005). Attachment as a cultural and ecological problem with pluralistic solutions. *Human Development, 48*, 89–94.

Wright, W. E. (2015). *Foundations for teaching English language learners: Research, theory, policy, and practice*. Philadelphia, PA: Caslon Publishing.

Chapter Six

Effective Literacy Instruction for English Learners

María Paula Ghiso

- Students' cultural and linguistic backgrounds are rich resources for the curriculum.
- Educators can create opportunities for literacy learning in school that draw on community knowledge.
- Effective literacy instruction is attentive to the larger social and political contexts of students' lives.

Laura patiently turned the pages on a Spanish-language workbook, pointing to the syllables as she read them aloud to her five-year-old son Julián. An immigrant from Peru, she had arrived in New York City several years earlier, but moved to suburban Indiana in the hopes of finding better schools for her son and a more affordable standard of living. Once there, Laura met with local educators and leaders to advocate for the creation of a dual language program that would benefit not only the nascent Latino community in her neighborhood, but also English-speaking children in becoming bilingual and biliterate.

Meanwhile, Laura continued to work diligently outside of school to teach her son to read and write in Spanish and about his Peruvian heritage. She faced obstacles such as nativist English-only sentiments and a standardized school curriculum that left little room for multilingualism and culturally relevant pedagogies. She also found allies in English to Speakers of Other Languages (ESOL) teachers who managed to work within and against the system to value her son's linguistic and cultural knowledge.

Despite Laura's successes, one tragic irony was that as she strived to support Julián's education in Spanish and English, her own family's first language, Quechua, was not being nurtured. Julián would possibly be the first generation in hundreds of years to not know the indigenous language of his ancestors.

Laura's story speaks to the many issues facing families and educators in their efforts to create literacy learning opportunities for multilingual students. While schools can compound the exclusion felt by many immigrant communities, educators also have tremendous power to act as advocates—to fashion classrooms where students' transnational identities and families' aspirations need not be left outside the door, but are central to academic achievement.

Suburban school districts across the country are rethinking their established programs and practices in order to be more attuned to the experiences of youth of immigrant backgrounds or who speak a language other than English at home (Wepner et al., 2012), and families are key partners in these endeavors. Like Laura, caregivers are mobilizing their cultural knowledge, multiple languages, and activist legacies to help make local schools more inclusive. This chapter offers guidelines for building on, and learning from, the cultural and linguistic resources of students and their families in the literacy curriculum.

TERMINOLOGY MATTERS

Who are the students who make up the frequently referenced "growing diversity" of suburban contexts? What do the labels we use make visible and what do they obscure? English language learner (ELL) and English learner (EL) are common ways of characterizing students who are acquiring English in school. This is an important shift away from limited English proficient (LEP) because it emphasizes the *process* of language and literacy learning rather than focusing on what students may "lack."

García (2009; see also García, Kleifgen, & Falchi, 2008) has advocated for using the term emergent bilingual (EB) to challenge the exclusive focus on English and to signal how all students who come into our schools speaking another language have the potential to become bilingual and biliterate. A number of students, like Laura's son Julián, might be considered emergent multilinguals (EMs).

Whatever the institutional term privileged in a given context, honoring bi/multilingualism reframes how students are viewed. In this era of accountability, there is increased attention to the academic performance of "subgroups," including those who speak a language other than English at home. Such metrics typically presume students' home languages to be a pedagogical challenge on the road to English literacy.

However, youth from immigrant backgrounds can also be thought of as "cosmopolitan intellectuals" (Campano & Ghiso, 2011) who "communicate in numerous languages, claim multiple identities, and have ties which extend beyond any one nation's borders" (p. 166). Literacy curricula call for teaching the twenty-first-century skills necessary to thrive in a more interconnected world, skills that many of the youth in our classrooms already possess. If "bilingualism, not monolingualism, is now the global norm" (Escamilla, 2009, p. 436), their transnational experiences can be sources of knowledge that edify the whole school community.

Beyond institutional categories, it is important to look at changing demographics within the specificity of local contexts. For example, some immigrant youth may have had the benefit of developing native-language literacy because of educational opportunities in their own countries, while others have experienced "interrupted" schooling due to political strife or economic disparities.

Immigrant students enter a racially stratified society, and may face discrimination related to their intersecting experiences around race, class, gender, religion, and immigration status (Campano, Ghiso, Yee, & Pantoja, 2013; Mangual Figueroa, 2012). Who students are, where they come from, the languages they speak, the literate legacies of their families, the details of their migratory and educational journeys, the sociopolitical context of their new homes in the United States, all these and many other factors influence how students engage with literacy in school, and the learning opportunities educators might provide for them.

LITERACY LEARNING, MULTILINGUALISM, AND POWER

While literacy involves the acquisition of particular skills, these skills for reading the word and the world (Freire, 1970) are not universal or neutral (Street, 1995) and vary cross-culturally.

- What might it mean, for example, to assess young children's concepts of print when in their own language system they may read from right to left or vertically? What assumptions are we in danger of making when an older EL structures an argumentative essay by leading with details and narrative as appropriate to the rhetorical style of his/her home country, rather than with the topic sentences common to U.S. schools?
- How would EB children respond to an assessment that requires sounding out decontextualized and "nonsense" words when it is the broader text that signals which of their multiple phonological systems to use?
- How can our understandings of family support expand beyond bedtime reading (Heath, 1982) to include storytelling traditions, reading and writing in religious spaces (like Sunday school or temple), neighborhood murals, and participation in activist organizations?

"What counts" as literacy within a given context can privilege particular practices and identities while marginalizing others.

ELs continually navigate a range of multilingual literacies to make competencies or literate artifacts like immigration papers that can demarcate national belonging.

Many children's academic struggles are related to the ways in which schools are (or are not) organized to recognize and leverage their cultural and linguistic resources. For example, a disproportionate amount of ELs and students of color have been tracked into special education (Artiles, Kozleski, Trent, Osher, & Ortiz, 2010), but that problem has less to do with their individual aptitudes and abilities than with what practices schools value.

Effective literacy instruction involves curricular strategies for strengthening academic reading and writing. They can go hand-in-hand with attending to the broader social contexts within which texts are used and interpreted (Janks, 2010). For example, educators can ask questions about how texts, genres, and languages can work to exclude, how authors' positionings influence the ideas they convey, and how texts might be reconstructed to be more inclusive and representative of the diversity of our schools and neighborhoods.

PROMISING PEDAGOGICAL PRACTICES FOR ELS/EMS

How, then, might educators cultivate spaces for literacy that are responsive to and informed by students' and families' funds of knowledge (González, Moll, & Amanti, 2005)? The next sections of this chapter describe promising pedagogical practices for ELs/EMs that create academic spaces for literacy learning within the context of children's languages, cultures, and community-based experiences (Ghiso, 2016; Ghiso, Martínez-Álvarez, & Dernikos, 2014; Martínez-Álvarez & Ghiso, 2014; 2015; Martínez-Álvarez, Ghiso, & Campano, 2014).

These promising practices are part of a research-based curriculum designed by Ghiso and Martínez-Álvarez that seeks to better connect school reading and writing with the transnational experiences of immigrant students. To help teachers acquire information about children's out-of-school interests and social and cultural worlds, photography was infused into literacy instruction. Students used low-cost digital cameras to photograph their neighborhoods and conduct video interviews with families, and these visual texts then became a platform for project-based reading and writing.

The project is an example of culturally relevant and sustaining pedagogy (Ladson-Billings, 1995; Paris, 2012) as the cultural resources of the children—their photographs, family stories, "community landmarks" in the neighborhood, multilingual literacies, and ethos of interdependence—became an integral part of their academic inquiries.

Using Children's Literature to Showcase Linguistic and Cultural Pluralism

Children's literature that highlights transnational experiences and the global social justice issues faced by immigrant groups is a rich instructional tool for situating the teaching of specific aspects of literacy within culturally relevant storylines. The benefit of students seeing themselves in books is well-established, as are the opportunities literature affords to learn about, and empathize with, the perspectives of others (Wolf, 2004; Wolf, Coates, Enciso, & Jenkins, 2011).

Children's literature can affirm classroom diversity (Nieto, 1992), help youth mobilize their cultural knowledge for inquiry (Martínez-Roldán, 2005), and foster critical discussions about situations that do not have ready-made answers, such as language hierarchy, racism, and family separation due to deportations (Ghiso & Campano, 2013; DeNicolo & Fránquiz, 2006). Picture books and young-adult literature can also underscore how diverse experiences may be braided together by shared histories of oppression and legacies of resistance (Ghiso, Campano, & Hall, 2012).

In the project described above, elementary school students read texts about being bilingual and bicultural that connected to the topics of inquiry they showcased in their photos. One example was *Dear Primo* by Duncan Tonatiuh (2010), a story of cousins Carlos and Charlie, one living in Mexico and one in the United States, who write letters to each other describing their respective sides of the border.

The book became the basis for instruction on determining the meaning of unfamiliar words, comparing and contrasting information, summarizing the multiple perspectives featured in the story, and deploying textual evidence to support literary interpretations. It also helped guide rich discussions on immigrant students' own cross-cultural experiences and their affinities and differences from those of the characters. Children commented on how they helped their parents with household responsibilities and caring for younger siblings just like Charlie helped his mother at the supermarket, but also challenged the exclusive portrayal of Mexico as rural by sharing stories of family members living in Mexico City.

Viewing Culture as Dynamic

When striving to diversify available literature portrayals and connect teaching objectives to the experiences of ELs/EBs, one must be cautious that these representations do not collapse into static or one-dimensional accounts.

Overly rigid assumptions about diverse identities can further marginalize students for not "fitting" within dominant cultural tropes or reduce their experiences to superficial markers like clothing, food, or holidays. Culture is dynamic and evolving (Rogoff, 2003). Language practices are similarly variable, with students and families moving across languages depending on the audience, topic, or context (García, 2009).

Educators, school leaders, and researchers have expressed the need to make instruction more culturally relevant to students' backgrounds. These efforts are most advantageous when one does not presume to know students' cultures from the onset. Alongside learning about their countries of origin and locating materials that speak to aspects of their identities, educators can make it a point to show a multiplicity of representations so as not to reify a "single story" (Adichie, 2009) of any one group.

Teachers can invite students to investigate how their cultures differ, overlap, and blend. They can feature a range of language varieties in the classroom, thus challenging hierarchies that cast some forms as more or less standard than others. They can launch classroom inquiries into what it means to identify as "Mexican," "Muslim," "immigrant," or "American," including the impact of how these categories are framed in public discourse. And they can be self-reflexive about their own identities, assumptions, and biases and how these shape their interactions with students.

Expanding What Counts as a "Text"

The dynamism of student populations and the landscape of how people use reading and writing in our increasingly networked world (The New London Group, 1996) make it necessary to think more broadly about the nature of "texts" and the practices used to engage with them. Scholars in multimodality have argued that "meanings are made (as well as distributed, interpreted, and remade) through many representational resources, of which language is but one" (Jewitt, 2008, p. 246; Kress & Van Leeuwen, 2001; Siegel, 2006). Images, sounds, gestures, and spatial layouts are all modes to convey and interpret messages that have a place in the school literacy curriculum alongside print.

EB children have rich funds of knowledge to add to the classroom, and drawing, gestures, or performance can add to their communicative repertoires. Incorporating visuals or movement (e.g., Total Physical Response) are common pedagogical strategies to make academic content comprehensible (Wright, 2015). A multimodal perspective treats meaning-making as more than "just" language; thus, visuals or gestures are not stepping stones to literacy (the means to an end), but are forms of literacy in and of themselves.

As Siegel (2012) argues,

> Even if we recognize the ways in which language and print literacy continue to serve as the power code . . . the potential of multimodal transformations to reframe students' school success and identities reminds us that this social arrangement is an effect of power and not the natural order of things. (p. 674)

Literacy is not neutral, but broadening which literacies count in classrooms can uncover and help mitigate power relations.

In Ghiso and Martínez-Álvarez's project, the children's photos became a platform for interpretation, analysis, and authorship. Applying the notion of "mentor texts" (Calkins, 1994) to a visual medium, students were invited to deconstruct the techniques photographers use to convey information. The children "read" the photographs of Latina/o photographers who explore their cultural communities and social justice themes in their work, examining what perspectives the author was communicating and how.

Students also engaged in small-group discussions around their selected images, used the photos to create digital comics, collaborated on a communal map of their neighborhood, and composed multimodal writings about topics of interest that fused photos, drawings, print in multiple languages, and three-dimensional paper art. They wrote more "traditional" informational and argumentative genre pieces shaped by the topics of their images and discussions. By alleviating the language demands of classroom instruction, these pedagogies provided openings for students to engage with complex content, learn reading strategies and writing techniques, and apply these to their own creations.

Valuing Oral Language as a Literate Practice

Speaking, listening, reading, and writing are intertwined and mutually informing processes. Scholars have long debunked theories that view literacy as the mark of economic and social progress and as more cognitively advanced than oral language practices (Street, 1995), what Graff (1991) has referred to as the "literacy myth."

Oral storytelling practices through which families pass on cultural knowledge to younger generations, for instance, are comprised of high-level vocabulary, story structure, and figurative language in forms compatible with school academic genres. The Latin American tradition of *testimonio* draws attention to the ways in which everyday people share stories to bear witness to injustice that may not be acknowledged in official texts or media.

ELs have a lot to contribute if educators invite their perspectives into the curriculum and structure classroom interaction in ways that facilitate communication. Students who are still gaining proficiency in the language of instruction benefit from opportunities to talk with one another in English and in their native languages. Being mindful of incorporating strategies such as increasing wait time, not overcorrecting errors, rephrasing and slowing down speech, and valuing all languages in the classroom encourages risk-taking and nurtures an inclusive learning community (Wright, 2016).

Honoring multilingual repertoires is not only the purview of bilingual educators. As Fránquiz and Reyes (1998) note, "A teacher does not have to be fluent in a language to recognize its value to the learner, permit its use in the classroom, and respect, affirm, and legitimize its role in students' learning and students' self-esteem" (p. 212). Storytelling practices can also be a pedagogical tool to support immigrant and nonimmigrant youth in connecting across cultural and racial divides (Enciso, 2011).

Building on Student Strengths to Support Academic Language Development

Oral language resources informed by students' cultures and out-of-school lives also have natural connections to what is commonly referred to as "academic language" (vocabulary, syntax, and genres) of disciplinary specific texts (Cloud, Genesee, & Hamayan, 2012; de Oliveira, 2011).

Orellana and colleagues (2003) examined how the frequent translating that immigrant children do outside of school (e.g., of legal notices, school letters, and financial statements) overlaps with academic tasks they are asked to undertake in school. Through their "paraphrasing" for families, they use their multilingual repertoires to figure out dense readings and convey the information in an accessible manner. As educators create opportunities for ELs to become familiar with the language and structure of different genres, it is important to remember that, far from "blank slates," students may already have experience with and strategies for comprehending complex texts.

In the project's photography and literacy inquiry, oral and academic languages were purposefully linked. Children spent extended time talking with one another about a chosen photograph in free-flowing ways. These conversations moved across English and Spanish as students discovered connections across their experiences and raised critical questions (Martínez-Álvarez et al., 2014). Students worked in pairs to analyze photos through an iPad notetaking app that did not just rely on print for communication: they could audio-record their intended messages and also draw on the images to signal what they were referencing (Martínez-Álvarez & Ghiso, 2014).

Listening to students' talk helped align literacy instruction with the issues the children discussed. For instance, the curriculum taught Tier 2 vocabulary (high-frequency content-area words) and strategies for figuring out unknown words through topics students' identified as salient. The teachers also tapped into children's critical dispositions by cultivating their ability to adjudicate among information presented in texts, think across sources, and link their community knowledge to academic content (Martínez-Álvarez & Ghiso, 2014).

Inquiring into Social Justice Issues

Beyond becoming adept at reading and writing skills, literacy entails using skills to better understand and act on the world around us. Literacy instruction can provide openings for children who are ELs/EMs to make visible their epistemic insights and reveal interests and concerns pertinent to their lives. This focus fosters engagement and educates the whole classroom community, as teachers and peers are able to learn about global issues, become exposed to other languages, writing systems, and storytelling traditions, and discover the affordances and challenges of families' migration journeys and day-to-day experiences.

In the process, educators may come to realize all that they did not know about the students in their classrooms. Through their discussions and writing in the project mentioned above, the ELs/EMs brought to the forefront issues absent from the school's mandated early literacy program, such as global mobility, economic disparities, or language policies. The Latina/o children had unique insights into inequality because of their transnational experiences and their vulnerability to social and economic precarity, which for many was exacerbated due to undocumented immigration status.

Thus, for example, many of the children were sensitized to relative wealth across countries, tense relationships with police, and the movement of goods and people across borders in ways that their teachers were not (Ghiso, 2016; Martínez-Álvarez et al., 2014). In contrast to deficit characterizations of Latina/o students' learning, by focusing their writing on these topics the children highlighted their expertise and agentively expanded the parameters of school literacies to accommodate their cultural values, interests, and real-world concerns.

Partnering with Families

More than anything, educators need to partner with families and community-based organizations around the education of language minority students. Like Laura, whose story opened this chapter, caregivers have invaluable insights into children's learning, dispositions, cultural identities, interests, and day-to-day experiences. They bring advocacy efforts for promoting bilingualism and biculturalism to neighborhood schools where language diversity is a new phenomenon. Families can also shed light on the intersecting factors that influence students' educational opportunities, such as the erosion of social supports and the effects of anti-immigrant sentiments that actively exclude, and often criminalize, those who speak a language other than English (Campano, Ghiso, & Welch, 2016).

Community organizations and local religious institutions strive to be "safer" spaces for immigrant populations—sites for congregation, cross-cultural sharing, programmatic resources such as ESL (English for Speakers of Other Languages) classes, and advocacy efforts for legislative and educational reform based on universal human dignity (Campano, Ghiso, Rusoja, Player, & Schwab, 2016).

Schools would do well to connect with organizations already serving the community to learn from their successes and forge mutually beneficial collaborations. These partnerships can help schools be in direct dialogue with immigrant families about their strengths, needs, and goals; coordinate educational offerings to build on already-existing resources; and infuse the curriculum with culturally relevant topics.

Engaging in Self-Reflexivity

In many school districts, language-minority students enter classrooms where they are seen as different by their peers, and are taught by predominantly monolingual-English, White educators. This can contribute to further entrenching "us" and "them" dichotomies that reinforce deficit perceptions of students and families, or it can be a profound learning opportunity. Engaging in self-reflexivity can make visible the ways educators' perspectives and practices are informed by their own social positions and work to strengthen bonds across cultural boundaries.

One pedagogical activity that links varied histories is an immigration timeline (Cho, Puente, Louie, & Khokha, 2004). This activity is a powerful tool for reflection among adults or with students as part of the literacy curriculum. Individuals draw and write about their own immigration backgrounds, whether these are recent memories or distant family histories. They then receive informational texts about immigration policies in the United States, beginning with the 1400s through the present day, and take turns reading aloud the facts and pasting them on the wall. The individual histories are then added to the corresponding period on the timeline.

This pedagogical approach situates particular stories within systemic issues that have shaped the experiences of immigrants historically, whether this migration was "voluntary" or forced through practices of slavery and the relocation of indigenous people. Common myths such as how earlier newcomers easily assimilated into American society or learned English more readily than current populations are challenged as participants reflect on the racialization of Irish and Italian immigrants now considered "White," the establishment of quotas through various legislative policies, and the institutionalization of English language hierarchies.

While employing literacy skills to access complex informational texts, students and teachers are also able to inquire how everyone is part of the immigration story, as well as come to understand their own privileges. "New" and "changing" populations within a town or school can be perceived by local residents as threatening. Literacy experiences like the immigration timeline can go a long way toward building bridges across difference and challenging misconceptions that too often "other" our neighbors.

CONCLUSION

And Laura and Julián? Their story took an unexpected turn during the recent economic recession. Laura's husband works as a truck driver, and the distances began taking a toll on his health. With the family struggling to make ends meet, they made the decision to live separately. Laura and the children, including Julián's younger, U.S.-born brother, moved to Peru, where they could live with her family and find work in the food industry. Her husband stayed behind, saving money to one day reunify the family.

While in Peru, Laura is using her digital literacy skills to keep the family connected across physical distances via Skype, and to access resources for tutoring her children in reading and writing in English while they attend a Spanish-language school. She is also tapping into networks for immigrant rights to help crowdfund her and her children's return to the United States.

The cosmopolitan practices of Laura, Julián, and so many others like them can inspire how suburban schools conceptualize the education of multilingual students in the literacy curriculum. Schools energized by global migrations and cultural flows (Appadurai, 1996) must contend with difficult challenges, including exclusionary policies, the prevalence of standardized curricula and the high-stakes evaluation system, and the host of out-of-school factors that shape children's educational opportunities. Despite this, they can find a way forward in the intellectual riches and collective agency of diverse twenty-first-century neighborhoods.

Literacy instruction for students who speak a language other than English need not be "either/or"—either learning the power codes of academic literacies in English or honoring students' home languages and community literacy practices. Rather, our pedagogies can contribute to a vision of education in a pluralistic society that is directed toward "both/and."

Educators can strive to transform both sides of the binary by supporting multilingual children and immigrant families in navigating schooling, and at the same time recreating the school literacy curriculum to have a more robust conception of community knowledge. One fruitful way of approaching this dual effort is through partnerships with caregivers, youth, and neighborhood leaders. This working ideal can surface dissonances but also enable individuals to make common cause toward visions of educational access and social change.

REFLECTION QUESTIONS

1. How might the experiences and identities of ELs help foster literacy instruction at school?
2. What do teachers have to learn about themselves and about their students in order to become more "effective"?
3. What is entailed in viewing the diversity of our changing suburbs as an intellectual opportunity rather than merely a challenge?

NOTE

Acknowledgments are extended to the Brooke Astor Fund for supporting the Photos and Me Program, and Alicia Rusoja for introducing the author to the immigration timeline.

REFERENCES

Adichie, C. (2009). *The danger of a single story*. Retrieved from http://www.ted.com/talks/chimamanda_adichie_the_danger_of_a_single_story?language=en

Appadurai, A. (1996). *Modernity al large: Cultural dimensions of globalization* (Vol. 1). Minneapolis, MN: University of Minnesota Press.

Artiles, A. J., Kozleski, E., Trent, S., Osher, D., & Ortiz, A. (2010). Justifying and explaining disproportionality, 1968–2008: A critique of underlying views of culture. *Exceptional Children, 76*(3), 279–299.

Calkins, L. (1994). *The art of teaching writing*. Portsmouth, NH: Heinemann.

Campano, G., & Ghiso, M. P. (2011). Immigrant students as cosmopolitan intellectuals. In S. Wolf, K. Coates, P. Enciso, & C. Jenkins (Eds.), *Handbook of research on children's and young adult literature* (pp. 164–176). New York, NY: Routledge.

Campano, G., Ghiso, M. P., Rusoja, A., Player, G., & Schwab, E. (2016). "Education without boundaries": Literacy pedagogies and human rights. *Language Arts, 94*(1), 43–53.

Campano, G., Ghiso, M. P., & Welch, B. (2016). *Partnering with immigrant communities: Action through literacy*. New York, NY: Teachers College Press.

Campano, G., Ghiso, M. P., Yee, M., & Pantoja, A. (2013). Community research and coalitional literacy practices for educational justice. *Language Arts, 90*(5), 314–326.

Cho, E. H., Puente, F. A. P., Louie, M. C. Y., & Khokha, S. (2004). *Bridge: Building a race and immigration dialogue in the global economy: A popular education resource for immigrant and refugee community organizers*. Oakland, CA: National Network for Immigrant and Refugee Rights.

Cloud, N., Genesee, F., & Hamayan, E. (2012). How do we promote English language learner's oral language development and use that as a foundation for academic language and literacy development? In R. Freeman Field & E. Hamayan (Eds.), *English language learners at school: A guide for administrators* (pp. 180–182). Philadelphia, PA: Caslon.

DeNicolo, C. P., & Fránquiz, M. E. (2006). "Do I have to say it?": Critical encounters with multicultural children's literature. *Language Arts, 84*(2), 157–170.

de Oliveira, L. C. (2011). *Knowing and writing school history: The language of students' expository writing and teachers' expectations*. Charlotte, NC: Information Age Publishing.

Enciso, P. (2011). Storytelling in critical literacy pedagogy: Removing the walls between immigrant and non-immigrant youth. *English Teaching, 10*(1), 21–40.

Escamilla, K. (2009). English language learners: Developing literacy in second-language learners—Report of the National Literacy Panel on Language-Minority Children and Youth: Book Review. *Journal of Literacy Research, 41*(4), 432–452.

Fránquiz, M. E., & Reyes, M. (1998). Creating inclusive learning communities through English language arts: From "chanclas" to "canicas." *Language Arts, 75*(3), 211–220.

Freire, P. (1970). *Pedagogy of the oppressed.* New York, NY: Continuum.

García, O. (2009). Emergent bilinguals and TESOL: What's in a name? *TESOL Quarterly 43*(2), 322–326.

García, O., Kleifgen, J. A., & Falchi, L. (2008). From English language learners to emergent bilinguals. Equity Matters. Research Review No. 1. *Campaign for Educational Equity, Teachers College, Columbia University.* Retrieved from http://files.eric.ed.gov/fulltext/ED524002.pdf

Ghiso, M. P. (2016). The laundromat as the transnational local: Young children's literacies of interdependence. *Teachers College Record, 118*(1), 1–46.

Ghiso, M. P., & Campano, G. (2013). Examining language ideologies in multilingual children's literature. *Bookbird, 51*(3), 47–55.

Ghiso, M. P., Campano, G., & Hall, T. (2012). Braided histories and experiences in literature for children and adolescents. *Journal of Children's Literature, 38*(2), 14–22.

Ghiso, M. P., Martínez-Álvarez, P., & Dernikos, B. (2014). Writing from and with community knowledge: First grade emergent bilinguals' engagement with technology-integrated curricula. In K. Pytash & R. Ferdig (Eds.), *Exploring technology for writing and writing instruction* (pp. 169–185). Hershey, PA: IGI Global.

González, N., Moll, L. C., & Amanti, C. (Eds.). (2005). *Funds of knowledge: Theorizing practices in households, communities, and classrooms.* Mahwah, NJ: Lawrence Erlbaum.

Graff, H. J. (1991). *The literacy myth: Cultural integration and social structure in the nineteenth century.* London, UK: Transaction Publishers.

Heath, S. B. (1982). What no bedtime story means: Narrative skills at home and school. *Language in Society, 11*(1), 49–76.

Janks, H. (2010). *Literacy and power.* New York, NY: Routledge.

Jewitt, C. (2008). Multimodality and literacy in school classrooms. *Review of Research in Education, 32,* 241–267.

Kress, G. R., & Van Leeuwen, T. (2001). *Multimodal discourse: The modes and media of contemporary communication.* London, UK: Arnold.

Ladson-Billings, G. (1995). Towards a theory of culturally relevant pedagogy. *American Educational Research Journal, 32*(3), 465–491.

Mangual Figueroa, A. (2012). "I have papers so I can go anywhere!": Everyday talk about citizenship in a mixed-status Mexican family. *Journal of Language, Identity & Education, 11*(5), 291–311.

Martínez-Álvarez, P., & Ghiso, M. P. (2014). Multilingual, multimodal compositions in technology-mediated hybrid spaces. In P. Fitzgerald (Ed.), *Digital tools for writing instruction in K–12 settings* (pp. 193–218). Hershey, PA: IGI Global.

Martínez-Álvarez, P., & Ghiso, M. P. (2015). On languaging and communities: Latino/a emergent bilinguals' expansive learning and critical inquiries into global childhoods. *International Journal of Bilingualism and Bilingual Education.* Retrieved from http://www.tandfonline.com/doi/full/10.1080/13670050.2015.1068270

Martínez-Álvarez, P., Ghiso, M. P., & Campano, G. (2014). Engaging double binds for critical inquiry with Latina/o emergent bilinguals. *Sustainable Multilingualism, 5,* 62–98.

Martínez-Roldán, C. M. (2005). The inquiry acts of bilingual children in literature discussions. *Language Arts, 83*(1), 22–32.

Nieto, S. (1992). *Affirming diversity: The sociopolitical context of multicultural education.* White Plains, NY: Longman.

Orellana, M. F., Reynolds, J., Dorner, L., & Meza, M. (2003). In other words: Translating or "para-phrasing" as a family literacy practice in immigrant households. *Reading Research Quarterly, 38*(1), 12–34.

Paris, D. (2012). Culturally sustaining pedagogy: A needed change in stance, terminology, and practice. *Educational Researcher, 41*(3), 93–97.

Rogoff, B. (2003). *The cultural nature of human development.* Oxford, UK: Oxford University Press.

Siegel, M. (2006). Rereading the signs: Multimodal transformations in the field of literacy education. *Language Arts, 84*(1), 65–77.

Siegel, M. (2012). New times for multimodality? Confronting the accountability culture. *Journal of Adolescent and Adult Literacy, 55*(8), 671–680.

Street, B. (1995). *Social literacies: Critical approaches to literacy in education, development and ethnography.* London, UK: Longman.

The New London Group. (1996). A pedagogy of multiliteracies: Designing social futures. *Harvard Educational Review, 66*(1), 60–93.

Tonatiuh, D. (2010). *Dear primo: A letter to my cousin.* New York, NY: Abrams Books for Young Readers.

Wepner, S. B., Ferrara, J. G., Rainville, K. N., Gómez, D. W., Lang, D. E., & Bigaouette, L. A. (2012). *Changing suburbs, changing students: Helping school leaders face the challenges.* Thousand Oaks, CA: Corwin Press.

Wolf, S. (2004). *Interpreting literature with children.* Mahwah, NJ: Lawrence Erlbaum.

Wolf, S., Coates, K., Enciso, P., & Jenkins, C. (2011). (Eds.). *Handbook of research on children's and young adult literature.* New York, NY: Routledge.

Wright, W. E. (2015). *Foundations for teaching English language learners: Research, theory, policy, and practice* (2nd ed.). Philadelphia, PA: Caslon.

Wright, W. E. (2016). Let them TALK! *Educational Leadership, 73*(5), 24–29.

Chapter Seven

Data-Driven Decisions on Effective Performance Measures of English Learners

Debbie Zacarian

- Common data need to be collected to identify, create, implement, and strengthen programming for English learners (ELs).
- Distinctions exist between ELs who (1) possess school-matched academic language and literacy skills and (2) do not yet possess these skills.
- Data decision practices need to be strengthened to more successfully meet the learning needs of all ELs.

This chapter explores three topics to strengthen what is being done to improve the outcomes of ELs. Strengthening this work is critical. ELs are one of the fastest-growing and complex groups in the United States. Unfortunately, they are also one of the most poorly performing in schools in the United States. Figure 7.1, which draws from the National Center for Education Statistics (2015), indicates that ELs are graduating at the lowest rate.

However, much can be done to draw from the inherent strengths and assets of culturally and linguistically diverse students and their families to make significant and lasting improvements. Below are examples of two five-year-old ELs who are enrolling in the same suburban school district for their first exposure to a formal education.

Example 1: Maria is a Spanish-speaking five-year-old EL from Mexico. She frequently observes her parents and grandmother reading newspapers, magazines, and other materials. She loves to imitate these tasks, and has plenty of books and an iPad to show them her emerging literacy interests. Her father is an architect and her mother is an electrical engineer.

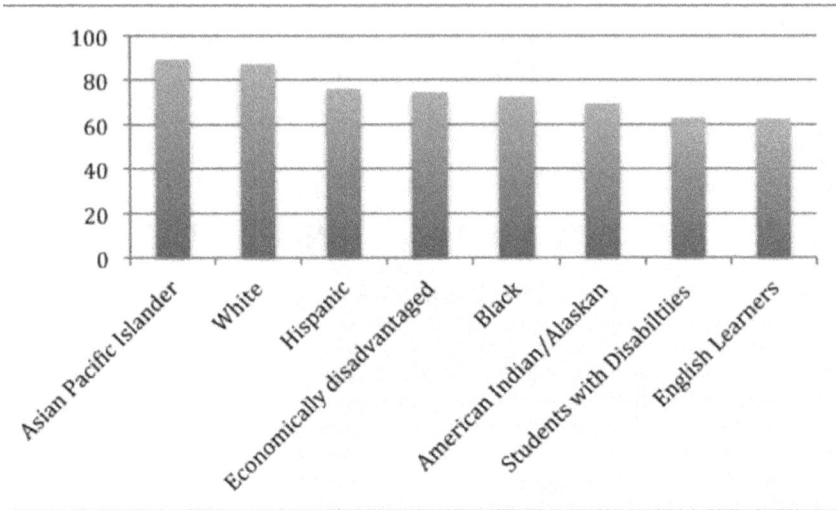

Figure 7.1. 2013–2014 U.S. Public School Graduation Rates

They completed their college education in Mexico. Her family (mother, father, and grandmother) moved from Mexico City to the United States, where her mother was transferred to work for the same international engineering company that she worked for in Mexico City. They have rented a home in a suburban community, and enrolled Maria in the local public school.

Example 2: Edwin is a Spanish-speaking five-year-old EL who, like Maria, is also from Mexico. Prior to moving to the United States, his family worked as farmers. They traveled wherever they found work migrating from one community to another in northern Mexico. His parents completed six years of schooling. Like the student in the first example, Edwin generally stays with his grandmother while his parents work. When she is not available, he sits alongside his parents while they work in the farming fields.

While this is occurring, he observes them closely and occasionally is allowed to assist them with their work. He loves it when he is called on to help. When this occurs, his parents explicitly direct his actions. At home, his parents and grandmother often recount stories about their childhood and the cultural community in which he is being reared. He loves these storytelling rituals, and can repeat many of them when asked. Recently, he moved with his parents and grandmother to the same suburban town as Maria so that his parents could continue their farming work. They enrolled Edwin in the same school as Maria. In it, the population of ELs has been increasing steadily for a number of years.

The following questions help to focus on ways to think about and assist Maria and Edwin:

1. What are some of the key similarities between Maria and Edwin?
2. What are some of the key differences between Maria and Edwin?
3. How might this information impact the decisions you might make about the educational programming that you would provide each of them?

IDENTIFYING ELS

Under federal laws and regulations (U.S. Department of Education, 1991), every district is required to: (1) identify its ELs, (2) notify parents/guardians when children are identified, and (3) describe the type of programming that their child will be provided to address his or her English language development needs. In practice, the most common means for determining potential ELs is asking parents to complete a home language survey followed by administering valid and reliable identification assessments when it is suspected that a child might be an EL.

When Maria's and Edwin's parents complete this survey, they respond that they and their children use Spanish exclusively to communicate. Following the laws and regulations, Maria and Edwin are then assessed and found to be ELs at the first or beginning stage of English language development. Figure 7.2 illustrates the process by which they, like all ELs in the nation, are identified.

COMMON DATA THAT ARE COLLECTED ABOUT ELS

The first reflection question about the similarities between Maria and Edwin brings to mind four main ideas. The first is the various language groups that are represented among ELs and that the two speak Spanish. In the United States, there are over 350 different languages spoken among the nation's ELs with Spanish being the most common (García, Jensen, & Scribner, 2009). The second idea is that there are various English language development levels of ELs and that the two are at the first stage. Every state in the United States provides English language development or proficiency-level standards that are intended to guide the thinking and practice with ELs.

The third idea is that there are various countries of origin of the two students. Both moved to the United States from Mexico. In some communities ELs represent over a hundred different countries of origin. In other communities all of its ELs hail from the same country. At the same time,

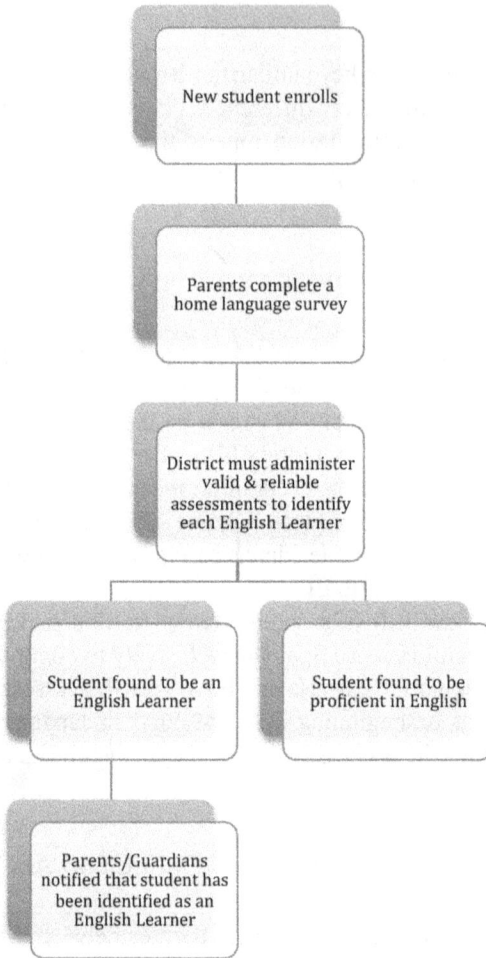

Figure 7.2. Identification Process

there are likely some communities of ELs that are born right here in the United States.

The fourth idea is the rapid growth of ELs in America's schools. Indeed, the percentage of public school ELs rose by 57 percent from 1995 to 2005 (Maxwell, 2009) and continues to grow (National Center for Education Statistics, 2014). This growth is reflected in Edwin and Maria's school district. Thus, they have a lot in common. Maria and Edwin are the same age, speak the same language, come from the same country, are at the same stage of

English language development, and attend the same school in a district with growing numbers of students like themselves—ELs.

Common data that most school districts collect about ELs include:

- home languages;
- countries of origin;
- levels of English language development/proficiency; and
- rate of growth in their respective districts/schools.

In addition, the following data are collected about ELs to determine how well programming is working:

- ELs' growth on state measures of English language development and on state assessments of English language arts and mathematics; and
- ELs' graduation rates.

While all of this is important information to collect (as federal laws and regulations require), outcomes must be closely analyzed, by asking "Why is it that some ELs are succeeding in school while others are not?" The response to this question helps to determine critical factors for strengthening students' success in learning English as a new or additional language.

To explore this further, the federal definition of an EL (U.S. DOE, n.d., Title IX General Provision 9101 [25]) is a student who is limited English proficient, and

> whose difficulties in speaking, reading, writing, or understanding the English language may be sufficient to deny the individual—
>
> a. the ability to meet the State's proficient level of achievement on State assessments described in section 1111(b)(3);
> b. the ability to successfully achieve in classrooms where the language of instruction is English; or
> c. the opportunity to participate fully in society.

This definition requires that students have the knowledge, skills, and competencies to do three things:

1. achieve at a level of proficient[1] on their state's assessments in English language arts and mathematics;
2. achieve at the same high level across all subject-matter disciplines (e.g., English, mathematics, science, and social studies); and
3. have the capacity to be an active and participatory member in their school, local community, and beyond.

In a real sense, these skills and capacities require that ELs possess the academic language and literacy skills needed for school success. In addition, and equally important, they should possess the contributory citizenry skills that are needed to be valued as a member in the society in which they participate.

URGENT CALL TO RETHINK THE DATA
COLLECTED TO MAKE DECISIONS

Given all of these differences in student populations, it is certainly *not* that all students from underrepresented groups do poorly in school, or that all students from dominant groups do well. Students who already possess school matched language and literacy skills at their grade level regardless of their family's income, language they speak, races they represent, or countries of origin have cracked the literacy code or school language code that is needed for school success.

Students such as these generally have had years of observing their family and community members using literacy. Further, they are reared in homes where school readiness and literacy practices are enacted regularly over and over and over again with the family's hope that their child will possess these language and literacy skills and carry them *like a literacy suitcase* from home, to school, in school, into the community, and so forth (Zacarian, 2013).

On the other hand, there are a number of students, such as Edwin, who do not yet possess these academic language or school language skills. While they are being reared in homes with caring, loving, and nurturing families, the focus of development is distinct from that of students who come from school-matched language experiences.

In addition to all of the differences discussed earlier as well as the common data used to form and analyze programming for ELs, one of the biggest concerns is students with school-matched language and literacy practices and those needing to learn them. Educators need to look at these differences more closely to capture the additional data that are sorely needed to strengthen what we do to improve students' outcomes.

DISTINCTIONS BETWEEN ACADEMIC LANGUAGE
AND LITERACY SKILLS OF ELS

There are major differences between students who already possess school language and literacy skills and those who do not yet possess these skills. Maria and Edwin highlight these differences. They enroll in the same kindergarten classroom in the suburban school district. They speak Spanish, are from the same country, and are at the first of five stages of English language development (what many refer to as beginning ELs).

Using these data, a likely decision might be to place the two in a program of English language development that is targeted to their beginning English language development needs. This is what commonly occurs across America. Unfortunately, this plan will not necessarily address their unique learning needs. To do that, educators have to look more carefully at the academic language and literacy differences between the two students. They also have to look closely at the ways in which support is given to all students to be participatory members in and valued members of their classrooms and beyond.

It is important to consider what all students generally experience during their development. All children use language to participate in the family and family community in which they are being reared (Gauvain, 2001). From birth forward, children observe language being used to communicate with others, are guided to use language both passively and actively through this exposure, and learn how to communicate through the range of rituals and routines to which they are repeatedly exposed (Zacarian & Silverstone, 2015).

Figure 7.3 illustrates the type of interactions that occur and expand during a child's development. A child is born. In general, the child first encounters and communicates with his or her parents/guardians. In a dynamically changing society, these might include two parents, a single parent, foster parents, adoptive parents, and more. The child then engages or interacts with family members. These include siblings, grandparents, and others. This is followed with the child's family's community such as the family's religious community and neighbors.

The child then goes to school, where he or she interacts with various teachers, peers, administrators, and others who make up the child's classroom and school community. As the child develops, these circles of interactions continuously grow and expand to include the local community and beyond (Zacarian & Silverstone, 2015).

While interactions are foundational for language development, there are important distinctions to consider between ELs who possess academic language and those who are learning academic language. In the following two sections, some of these distinctions are discussed.

Students with Academic Language

Maria is a student who already possesses school-matched language skills, and carries them like a well-equipped *literacy suitcase* wherever she goes (Zacarian, 2013). Looking a little deeper at some of the practices that she has been exposed to since birth, it becomes obvious why she already possesses

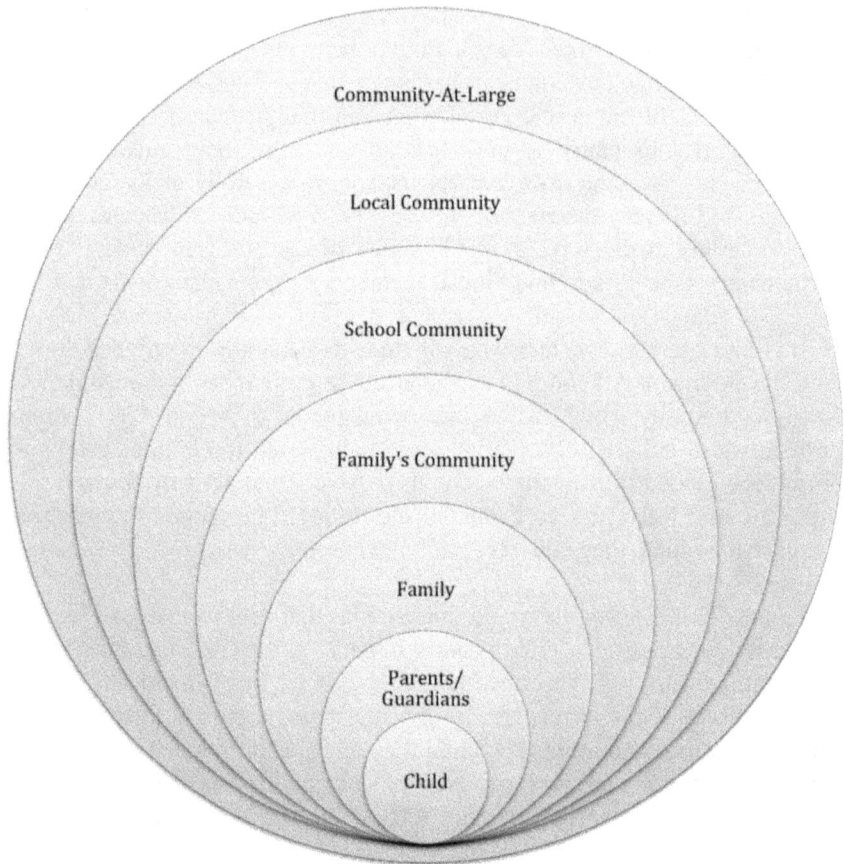

Figure 7.3. Circles of Interactions

school-matched language and literacy skills. First, her parents are formally educated, and have an extensive vocabulary with which to communicate (Hart & Risley, 1995; Heath, 1983). Indeed, they are familiar with school-based practices because they have experienced it themselves repeatedly throughout their childhood and early adult years when they completed their elementary, secondary, and college educations.

Since birth, Maria has observed her parents reading the local newspaper, books for pleasure, and recipe books. She has seen them make lists of things to do, and make decisions and take actions that are targeted to advancing their quality of life. Examples of this are navigating what is needed for job/career advancement, making health decisions about diet and exercise, and investigating economic and academic prospects. Maria's understanding of the world around her is being strengthened, reinforced, and encouraged by these practices (Pransky, 2008; Rogoff, 1990; Zacarian, 2011; 2013). That is, their child-rearing practices support her building the academic- and language-readiness skills that she needs for school success and more.

There are important elements at play here that are worthy of discussing. Zwiers, O'Hara, and Pritchard (2014) and Delpit (1995) refer to the type of foundational language rearing that her parents are engaging as matching the same type of language and literacy that she will be exposed to and required to use in school. In fact, they interact with Maria in ways that are familiar to many, if not all, educators.

For example, when Maria's parents take her to the local aquarium, where she sees a big shark tank, they ask her questions about the sharks. "Why do you think the sharks have such big teeth?" Her parents act as *coaches*. They do not furnish her with the answer to their query. Rather, they use a type of language practice that parallels what occurs in school. They ask open-ended questions with the expectation that she will use her own independent thinking skills to determine a possible response.

If Maria points to one of the sharks and says, "That big shark has big teeth because he eats a lot," her parents ask another open-ended question such as, "Why do you think he eats a lot?" Each of these exchanges helps Maria to think independently. Indeed, this is a goal that they have for their child. They want to prepare her for the future as a learner in school. These behaviors parallel what is expected of students in school—to think independently as a learner.

The same holds true for the types of exchanges that they might have around mealtime. Her parents might go into an area of their home where she is playing with blocks, a toy car, or a handheld device such as an iPad, or is watching television. They say, "It's lunchtime." What does it mean? It is an unspoken directive to stop doing what she is doing, wash her hands, and come to the table prepared to eat. They expect that she will respond by following this sequence of events because they have supported her in developing the behavioral and cognitive skills that are needed to self-regulate.

Indeed, this, too, is an example of the many skills expected of students in school. Teachers want them to be self-regulatory. They are expected to have the executive function skills needed to engage successfully in a variety of situations. For example, in Maria's classroom, her kindergarten teacher enacts the same type of unspoken directive with a clap of the hands, flick of the lights, or an open hand indicating stop to signal the following: stop doing what you are doing, get ready to make a transition, and make the transition.

Thus, before a child such as Maria steps foot in school, he or she has been reared in a home with rich vocabulary, a literacy culture, activities that require the same type of sequencing and organizational skills that will be required in school, and what it means to think as an independent learner. In addition, these children are engaging in the same dialect and language practices that are used in school (Delpit, 1995; Heath, 1983; Pransky, 2008; Zacarian, 2011; 2013). As such, parents are supporting children in developing a language system that matches what is used in school, and is needed for school success and beyond.

Students Learning Academic Language

The second student, Edwin, is being reared in a home culture and community that is different from Maria. First, Edwin's parents have less formal education. While they have a rich language and vocabulary with which to communicate, it is in a dialect that is distinct from the one used in school (Delpit, 1995; Hart & Risley, 1995; Heath, 1983). It is most frequently described as vernacular or informal language (Labov, 2006).

Second, he is being reared in a *collectivist culture*. In a collectivist culture, interdependence, interconnectedness, and group harmony are highly valued (DeCapua & Marshall, 2011; Hofstede, 2001; Hofstede & Hofstede, 2005). Families from collectivist cultures place a high value on their relationships to and membership in their cultural community, which includes a close and explicit adherence to the community's rules, routines, and behaviors.

In this sense, the sociocultural focus of childrearing is on community needs versus individual needs, or in doing what is best for the good of the community versus the advancement of an individual's goals. Indeed, a hallmark of a collectivist culture is a belief that the community's well-being takes precedence over an individual's.

To support Edwin's standing as an active member of their community, his parents are explicit in directing him in daily routines and practices. Rules are explicitly taught and enacted to ensure adherence to them in their collectivist cultural community. For example, when it is time for Edwin to eat, they go to their son, bring him to their washroom, help him wash his hands, and then bring him to the table. They do not expect him to think independently. Rather, they ensure that their son enacts behaviors that are expected of him by helping him to do them.

According to Bailey and Pransky (2014), there is research that shows a difference in the development of executive function skills between students who carry academic language and those learning academic language. Students such as Maria have had years and years of support to develop executive functioning skills. Her interactions at home and in school reinforce this continuous growth toward being a self-regulatory, independent learner. Students such as Edwin require explicit, direct support in developing, internalizing, and using these essential skills at will.

STRENGTHENING PRACTICE TO MEET THE ACADEMIC LANGUAGE LEARNING NEEDS OF ELS

Two major government-funded meta-reviews of research about successful practices for ELs (August & Shanahan, 2006; Genesee, Lindholm-Leary, Saunders, & Christian, 2006) found that they must include:

- models of instruction that are explicitly connected to students' personal, social, cultural, world, and language backgrounds; and
- systematic and explicit development of the type of language and literacy that is needed for school success.

As district and school educators work with and collect data about ELs who (1) carry academic language and (2) are learning academic language, they have to think about English as a second or additional language and literacy learning as a four-pronged interdependent process (August & Shanahan, 2006; Collier, 1995; Genesee et al., 2006; Zacarian, 2011; 2012; 2013). That is, academic language learning is a:

1. sociocultural process that must be connected to students' prior personal, social, cultural, and world experiences;
2. developmental process that must factor in students' various levels of English language and literacy development;
3. subject matter or academic learning process that must be explicitly built and instructed from students' prior academic learning experiences; and
4. cognitive process in which explicit direct instruction on how students should think as learners is provided.

To incorporate all four processes requires a belief that interactions are critical for academic language learning. The more educators draw information available from students' circles of interactions, the more opportunities can be provided for them to learn. Further, the data collected for improving the outcomes of ELs must come by examining the ways in which learning through interactions is encouraged. An optimal atmosphere is required and can only happen when all students' strengths and assets are acknowledged, valued, and used.

Carol Dweck (2014), a renowned psychologist in motivation, provides some important insights. These include that the distinctions between individualist and collectivist cultures are important considerations. She cites a study of Native Americans where teachers tried to motivate students, unsuccessfully, by asking them to focus on doing their personal best (e.g., do well on tests and report cards). Teachers learned that this type of motivational focus matched students from individualistic cultures as opposed to the collectivist group that these students represented.

What did the teachers do? They began using a collectivist approach by explicitly showing students ways in which their performance in class would benefit their home communities. It resulted in students' performance improving remarkably.

Her findings point to the importance of building from and capitalizing on students' cultural ways of being and acting. These can be made much more meaningful when they are also connected to the circles of interactions that all students have available to them. For example, families are powerful resources when school personnel take time to build relationships with them and connect students' learning to them. An example of this is the findings of researchers Moll, Amanti, Neff, and Gonzalez (1992).

They studied the expertise that all families bring to their child's learning. They researched a group of families living in a border region between the United States and Mexico. While some might refer to the families using deficit-based language (e.g., *semiliterate*), they found that the families possessed very high levels of knowledge related to their work and home life, and had a strong sense of well-being that they passed on to their children.

Moll and colleagues (1992) coined the term *funds of knowledge* to describe the rich resources that families can bring to their child's learning *when* teachers see these as strengths and intentionally infuse these into their practice. An important step to creating, planning, and implementing instruction and making data-based decisions is ensuring that they are connected to students' home/family experiences. There are endless possibilities for ensuring that this occurs.

It requires making connections between learning and experiences that draw from the *circles of interactions* illustrated in figure 7.3 between students and their families, students and their families' community, school community, local community, and community at large. Also, it involves honoring, valuing, and acknowledging students and their families, including the various languages that they speak, dialects they use, and their varied personal, cultural, social, and world experiences.

Further, it necessitates focused attention on the four processes of learning academic language as a sociocultural, developmental, academic, and cognitive process. This includes the processes that explicitly and directly support students in developing the executive functioning skills needed to self-regulate, self-direct, and think critically as learners. Here is an example of what this looks like in practice.

Example in Practice

Edwin and Maria, the focal students in this chapter, are students in Mrs. Pratt's kindergarten class. Knowing that many of the families represent collectivist cultures, Mrs. Pratt and her colleagues have taken time to build relationships with families. They have held a number of activities to do this, including potluck suppers, family picnics, game nights, and class plays. All of these have occurred for the sole purpose of building relationships. Many families, including Maria's and Edwin's, attend these events.

Mrs. Pratt has also built relationships with each of her students. She knows each of their interests and draws from these to build her lessons. Edwin, for example, loves to play soccer. Maria loves to dance. Many of the books that she selects for each to read represent their personal interests. She is also aware of the English language development levels of each of her ELs, and targets her instruction to these levels. Additionally, one of her key goals is that students will learn how to use language to express their thinking.

Mrs. Pratt is currently teaching a social studies unit titled "Why People Move from One Place to Another." Drawing from the important circles of interactions, she asks students to interview their families or families' friends about why they moved from one location to another. She sends a note home, in Spanish, letting families know what the students are studying, and asks a translator to contact families about this assignment. Students go home and ask their families or friends of their families the question. Mrs. Pratt also invites various members of the students' school, family, and local communities to her class to discuss why they moved to the local community.

She explicitly teaches her students how language is used to express their findings. One strategy that she uses, for example, is the sentence starter "A reason that people moved here is _____." She provides an example response such as "A reason that people move here is to be near family." She explicitly teaches her students to use a specific graphic or visual organizer to describe their findings (e.g., a Venn diagram to display similarities and differences).

Mrs. Pratt also requires students to engage in working cooperatively in pairs and small groups as it matches the collectivist cultures of many of her students. For example, in pairs and small groups, students discuss the common reasons that people move. Each small group of students selects one visual organizer to display findings and uses this to create a poster presentation of the group's learning. The students invite families as well as the members from their school and local communities who contributed to their studies to attend the presentations.

Throughout these experiences, Mrs. Pratt collects data about her students' participation in the various interactive tasks and activities. For example, as Maria's and Edwin's small groups engage in the explicit tasks that she assigns, she notes their interactions. She also collects data about parents' participation in the various events that are held. She notes that Maria's and Edwin's parents attend the potluck supper.

However, she also notes that Edwin's parents do not seem to interact with other families. She is now seeking ways to bolster their interactions with others in school settings. All of these activities are targeted at strengthening her students' engagement in their learning communities as well as their performance in school.

CONCLUSION

There are many conventions for collecting data and scaling up students' interactions to learn and be engaged members of their learning communities. Examples are found in *Mastering Academic Language: A Framework for Supporting Student Achievement* (Zacarian, 2013) and *In It Together: How Student, Family, and Community Partnerships Advance Engagement and Achievement in Diverse Classrooms* (Zacarian & Silverstone, 2015). Regardless of the instruments used, when attention focuses on increasing the circles of interactions as well as the four processes for learning academic language that have been presented, there is a chance of strengthening students' performance. Moving in this direction is essential to better ensure that students flourish in classrooms and beyond. And there is no better or more urgent time to do this than right now.

REFLECTION QUESTIONS

1. What are the typical data that are collected to identify, create, implement, and strengthen programming for ELs?
2. Why is it critical to understand and build programming based on the key differences between ELs who (1) possess school-matched academic language and literacy skills and (2) do not yet possess these skills?
3. What can be done to strengthen data-collection practices to more successfully meet the needs of the changing EL populations by drawing from their strengths and assets?

NOTE

1. According to the National Assessment of Educational Progress (NAEP) (2010), student performance on state assessments is measured according to three levels, including basic, proficient, and advanced.

REFERENCES

August, D., & Shanahan, T. (Eds.). (2006). *Executive summary: Developing literacy in second-language learners: Report of the National Literacy Panel on Language-Minority Children and Youth*. Mahwah, NJ: Lawrence Erlbaum.

Bailey, F., & Pransky, K. (2014). *Memory at work in the classroom: Strategies to help underachieving students*. Alexandria, VA: Association for Supervision and Curriculum Development.

Collier, V. (1995). Acquiring a second language for school. *Directions in Language Education, 1*(4), 1–8. Retrieved from http://www.usc.edu/dept/education/CMMR/CollierThomas_Acquiring_L2_for_School

DeCapua, A., & Marshall, H. W. (2011). *Breaking new ground: Teaching students with limited or interrupted formal education in U.S. secondary schools*. Ann Arbor, MI: University of Michigan Press.

Delpit, L. (1995). *Other people's children: Cultural conflict in the classroom*. New York, NY: New Press.

Dweck , C. (2014, November). *The power of believing that you can improve* [Video file]. Retrieved from http://www.ted.com/talks/carol_dweck_the_power_of_believing_that_you_can_improve?language=en

García, E. E., Jensen, B. T., & Scribner, K. P. (2009). Supporting English language learners. *Educational Leadership, 66*(7), 8–13. Washington, DC: Association for Supervision and Curriculum Development.

Gauvain, M. (2001). *The social context of cognitive development*. New York, NY: Guilford Press.

Genesee, F., Lindholm-Leary, K., Saunders, W., & Christian, D. (2006). *Educating English language learners*. New York, NY: Cambridge University Press.

Hart, B., & Risley, T. (1995). *Meaningful differences in the everyday experience of young American children*. Baltimore, MD: Brookes.

Heath, S. B. (1983). *Ways with words: Language, life, and work in communities and classrooms*. Cambridge, UK: Cambridge University Press.

Hofstede, G. (2001). *Culture's consequences: Comparing values, behaviors, institutions, and organizations across nations* (2nd ed.). Thousand Oaks, CA: Sage.

Hofstede, G., & Hofstede, G. J. (2005). *Cultures and organizations: Software of the mind* (2nd ed.) New York, NY: McGraw Hill.

Labov, J. (2006, March). *Unendangered dialects, endangered people*. Paper presented at Georgetown University Round Table on Languages and Linguistics, Washington, DC. Retrieved from http://www.ling.upenn.edu/~wlabov/Papers/UDEP.pdf

Maxwell, L. A. (2009, January 6). Shifting landscape: Immigration transforms communities. *Education Week, 28*(17), 10–11.

Moll, L., Amanti, C., Neff, D., & Gonzalez, N. (1992). Funds of knowledge for teaching: Using a qualitative approach to connect homes and classrooms. *Theory into Practice, 31*(2), 132–141.

National Assessment of Educational Progress. (2010). *Comparing NAEP and state assessments*. Retrieved from http://nces.ed.gov/nationsreportcard/about/comparing_assessments.aspx

National Center for Education Statistics. (2014). *Number and percentage of public school students participating in programs for English language learners, by state: Selected years, 2002-03 through 2012-13*. Retrieved from https://nces.ed.gov/programs/digest/d14/tables/dt14_204.20.asp

National Center for Education Statistics. (2015). *Common core of data [CCD]*. Retrieved from https://nces.ed.gov/ccd/tables/ACGR_RE_and_characteristics_2013-14.asp

Pransky, K. (2008). *Beneath the surface: The hidden realities of teaching culturally and linguistically diverse young learners K–6*. Portsmouth, NH: Heinemann.

Rogoff, B. (1990). *Apprenticeship in thinking: Cognitive development in social context*. New York, NY: Oxford University Press.

Sage Publication. (2015). *Corwin TeachALL* (Version 1.0.1). [Mobile application software]. Retrieved from https://itunes.apple.com/us/app/corwin-teachall/id979821890?mt=8

U.S. Department of Education. (n.d.). *Title IX general provision 9101 (25)*. Retrieved from http://www2.ed.gov/policy/elsec/leg/esea02/pg107.html

U.S. Department of Education. (1991). *Policy update on schools' obligations toward national origin minority students with limited-English proficiency*. Retrieved from http://www2.ed.gov/about/offices/list/ocr/docs/lau1991.html

Zacarian, D. (2011). *Transforming schools for English learners: A comprehensive framework for school leaders*. Thousand Oaks, CA: Corwin Press.

Zacarian, D. (2012). *Serving English learners: Laws, policies, and regulations*. Colorincolorado.com. Retrieved from http://www.colorincolorado.org/sites/default/files/Policy_Guide_Final.pdf

Zacarian, D. (2013). *Mastering academic language: A framework for supporting student achievement*. Thousand Oaks, CA: Corwin Press.

Zacarian, D., & Silverstone, M. A. (2015). *In it together: How student, family and community partnerships advance engagement and achievement in diverse classrooms*. Thousand Oaks, CA: Corwin Press.

Zwiers, J., O'Hara, S., & Pritchard, R. (2014). *Common core standards in diverse classrooms: Essential practices for developing academic language and disciplinary literacy*. Portland, ME: Stenhouse.

Chapter Eight

Closing the Parent Gap in Changing School Districts

Patricia A. Edwards, Lisa Domke, and Kristen White

- Suburban schools must challenge traditional notions of parental involvement.
- School districts must promote an inclusive school climate and view families with an asset-based perspective.
- All families need access to classroom ideas and an understanding of school requirements and procedures.

The idyllic scenario of living in a neighborhood with perfectly manicured lawns, white picket fences, and good schools is what many Americans dream for themselves. The rapid suburbanization over the last several decades has been driven, in part, by the belief that this dream is attainable in the suburbs. The nation's suburbs have grown much more diverse over the past generation, as Blacks and Hispanics have followed Whites out of cities and into surrounding areas (Badger, 2014; Drayton, 2015).

Many suburban school districts nationwide are experiencing rapid growth in the number of students of color, culturally and linguistically diverse students, and students from low-income families. Unfortunately, these diverse groups are still likely to live in neighborhoods where they are isolated from Whites, regardless of income. And those neighborhoods are likely to have more poverty and lower-performing schools than the suburban neighborhoods where Whites live, suggesting that economic, racial, and power inequalities are replicating themselves in the suburbs (Badger, 2014; Drayton, 2015).

Oftentimes, teachers and administrators deplore the lack of visibility, the disengagement, and the detachment of diverse parents' presence in schools and participation in school activities. Repeatedly, they question whether diverse parents care about the educational success of their own children, or if they promote the importance of learning outside of school contexts (Fields-Smith, 2005; Noguera, 2001; Yan, 2000).

Rural, suburban, and urban schools alike theoretically support the notion of parental involvement as an essential component to the educational success of students (Boutte & Johnson, 2013). Although the benefits of parental involvement are evident to educators, there is still a lack of knowledge as to how parent involvement may be shaped by the type of school setting. Urban, suburban, and rural school districts each have a unique set of characteristics and obstacles that may impact the degree of family involvement (Prater, Bermudez, & Owens, 1997).

Frequently, the issue of understanding and recognizing diverse parents' lack of visibility in schools is clouded by deficit views. According to Howard (2007),

> Some teachers, administrators, and parents view their schools' increasing diversity as a problem rather than an opportunity. Some teachers and administrators have asked, "Why are they sending these kids to our school? . . . These kids don't value education, and their parents aren't helping either. They don't seem to care about their children's future." (p. 16)

Too often, schools view parents' disengagement as a fixed or natural practice without considering the structural and systemic inequities families face (Johnson, 2015). However, Howard (2007) posits that diversity-enhanced school districts are places of vibrant opportunity that call educators to meaningful and exciting work. He contends that "in these 'welcome-to-America' schools, the global community shows up in our classrooms every day, inviting us—even requiring us—to grow as we learn from and with our students and their families" (p. 16). In other words, *all* families bring assets and cultural capital.

Educators in rapidly transitioning, diversity-enhanced schools need to reexamine everything they do. Educational leaders are moving beyond blame and befuddlement, and are trying to transform themselves and their schools to serve all their students and families. Educational leaders and teachers must be willing to develop new competencies and pedagogies to successfully engage changing student populations, confront current and historical inequities that affect education, form authentic and caring relationships with students, use curriculum that honors each student's culture and life experiences, and shift instructional strategies to meet diverse learners' needs (Howard, 2007).

This chapter discusses ways of (re)conceptualizing parental and family involvement that confront inequities. It describes ways to build an inclusive climate that establishes trust and engages the community and its cultures. It also describes how to increase school access by improving communication and breaking down structural barriers.

SHIFTING DEMOGRAPHICS: (RE)CONCEPTUALIZING PARENTS AND AN INCLUSIVE CLIMATE

While urban schools warrant continued attention, so too do suburban schools located outside city limits (Gill, Posamentier, & Hill, 2016). Often receiving less notice, suburban schools also face economic challenges and may not be equipped to handle the changing demographics that typically characterize large cities. Kneebone and Berube (2013) found "populations living below the federal poverty line grew twice as fast between 1970 and 2010 in suburbs as in cities, almost three times as fast between 2000 and 2012" (p. 19). A first step in meeting these dynamic demographic shifts is reconsidering the school's role (Edwards, 2016).

The challenge is to rethink how schools conceptualize and define *parent(s)* and *parental engagement*. Institutions have held traditional views of parents in a child's life. However, it is crucial to consider how labels like *parents* may unintentionally exclude other important people from supporting children in educational settings. Alternatively, the term *caregivers*, which includes, but is not limited to, extended family members, neighbors, friends, and foster parents, broadens traditional roles of those involved in a child's education, contributing to an inclusive and effective home-school partnership.

Caregivers' involvement in a child's education influences not only educational outcomes (Edwards, 2016; Goldenberg, 2001; Milner, 2015; Whitehurst & Longigan, 2002) but also social success in school. However, a one-size-fits-all approach to caregivers' involvement will not increase students' academic success (Robinson & Harris, 2014). To better meet the needs of a progressively diverse population, school and district staff need to reconsider caregiver engagement by first asking, "Is the school climate friendly for all caregivers?"

CREATING A DEMOGRAPHIC PROFILE AND WELCOMING ATMOSPHERE FOR CAREGIVERS

The first suggestion to increase inclusivity is to generate a demographic profile of the caregivers in a school context (see Edwards, 2004; 2009). A *demographic profile* "is a composite description of the parent community that exists in your school building, as well as in individual classrooms" (Edwards, 2016, p. 7). Understanding who makes up the community will assist in creating a caregiver-friendly environment that meets local needs.

Research suggests that children from diverse backgrounds perform better in school when families and schools work together to bridge the gap between home and school cultures (Henderson & Mapp, 2002).

The Iowa Parent Information Resource Center (2008) describes a *welcoming* atmosphere in a school where families feel at home, comfortable, and as though they belong to the school community. The suggestion is for educators to assess how they familiarize caregivers with the school and its staff. Similarly, Underhill (n.d.) of *PTO Today* asserts that openness is a crucial element in schools with diverse cultures. "How to Evaluate Your School" is a helpful resource that schools can use to assess whether they have an open or caregiver-friendly environment (see https://www.ptotoday.com/pto-today-articles/article/398-is-your-school-parent-friendly).

Several states (e.g., Indiana, Iowa, and Ohio) have developed assessment tools for schools seeking to improve caregiver engagement. For example, the Iowa Parent Information Resource Center (2008) offers five comprehensive tools that assess school–caregiver partnerships across five different areas: building relationships, linking to learning, addressing differences, supporting by advocacy, and sharing power (access assessments at http://www. heartlandaea.org/media/documents/Parent_Friendly_Schools_ E52DE9605B233.pdf).

Schools can demonstrate openness by soliciting the help of several caregivers from diverse cultures in assessing the school's overall friendliness. Recruiting various caregivers across racial and ethnic lines increases inclusivity and ensures that the school openly values opinions representative of the entire community instead of only a select few. The variety of perspectives not only invites caregivers who might be reluctant to participate on their own, but may also help establish relationships between existing families and those families new to the school or those who may not feel comfortable in the school.

Once a school completes a demographic profile, data analyses can begin along with an evaluation of how welcoming the school is. Underhill (n.d.) recommends that teams of four to five people assess a particular area related to welcoming (e.g., school staff, physical environment, written materials, practices and policies) and share the results. Using the results, the school can develop an action plan to address areas of welcoming that need improvement to build a more inclusive and friendly school climate. The ultimate goal is to increase caregiver engagement and students' academic and social success.

ASSESSING STUDENTS' AND FAMILIES' NEEDS

The second suggestion to increase inclusivity is to determine students' and families' needs. This should follow the demographic profile and the assessment of the school environment for welcoming caregivers. Some students are *school dependent* because they rely on school for basic needs such as meals, academic support, and exposure to museums and other learning opportunities outside the traditional classroom. Some caregivers also depend on the school to enlist community members and groups to offer students extra support and resources (Milner, 2015). It is important to ask caregivers how the school can best meet their needs.

One way schools might seek information about caregiver needs is through a survey or home visit. If families speak a language other than English, the survey must be either translated in written form or presented orally in the native language(s) of the caregivers. Additionally, a home visit would require a translator if the caregivers and the visitors do not speak the same language. A survey with a few basic questions can help the school become aware of familial and caregiver needs and make decisions about ways to deploy resources to meet such needs. Below are a few sample questions:

1. Is the school meeting your needs? What is and is not working? Is there anything the school or teachers can do to help your child be successful in school?
2. What would you like us to know about your child? What does he or she like to do? What doesn't he or she like to do?
3. How can we best serve your family? What can we do to help your child and your family succeed in school and the community?

After the school has compiled the survey responses, it can establish a list of priorities for addressing unmet needs and requests. This is a ripe opportunity to establish connections and partnerships with the surrounding community. For example, a school can enlist professional coaches and athletes, local political leaders, the Boys and Girls Club, the United Way, recreation centers, the library, churches, synagogues, and mosques as resources (Milner, 2015). Additionally, schools can recruit and train local and willing community members such as social workers, clergy, coaches, and high school National Honor Society members to serve as mentors and role models.

DIFFERENTIATED INVOLVEMENT

The third suggestion is to recognize and provide *differentiated parenting involvement* opportunities (Edwards, 2004; 2009; 2016). Each community is rich with resources, but engaging diverse caregivers requires educators' time, commitment, and a mindset to do the necessary work. This includes recognizing and embracing the differences among caregivers' needs.

By doing so, educators develop an attitude of differentiated parenting, similar to the ways in which teachers provide differentiated instruction by tailoring teaching to meet individual students' needs. For caregivers, this means ensuring that the ways in which schools engage with caregivers are *parentally appropriate* so that their individual capabilities and strengths are considered when developing expectations and planning activities.

Research has shown that (1) one way does not exist for all caregivers to be successfully involved in their children's schooling; (2) not all forms of caregiver involvement result in improved student achievement; and (3) the effects of some involvement activities are not the same across races/ethnicities or social classes (Robinson & Harris, 2014). Traditional methods of caregiver involvement such as attending Parent Teacher Organization/Association meetings or ice cream socials, volunteering, or even helping with homework do not guarantee school success. Instead, one of the most important things caregivers can do is communicate to their children, early and often, the value of schooling.

Thus, involvement that places caregivers' needs along with student achievement at the forefront requires that schools restructure expectations and activities. Educators must adopt the mantra that all children, families, and communities have assets upon which the school can build. They must *listen* to the school population to build understanding and trust. Next, they must develop a plan to meet caregivers' needs and foster students' academic achievement. This not only creates an improved school climate, but also leads to improved school access for caregivers.

IMPROVING ACCESS

Meeting caregivers' needs and making them feel welcome entails more than posting signs around the school in multiple languages, though it is an important start. The fourth suggestion is to examine school personnel's mindsets. López, Scribner, and Mahitivanichcha (2001) studied Texan schools' support of migrant students' academic achievement (i.e., students whose families frequently move within and between countries often to follow agricultural jobs) and found that

> unlike other research which identifies a welcoming environment by the physical surroundings of the school (e.g., brightly colored bulletin boards, welcome banners, etc.), our research suggests that school personnel in these districts understood this concept as rooted in one's attitude and demeanor toward parents. (p. 272)

Not only must school personnel (re)conceptualize who the caregivers are and promote a more inclusive school climate for them, but in order to increase access and create a welcoming atmosphere, school personnel must also be open-minded and view caregivers from an asset-based perspective instead of a deficit view.

Asset-Based Perspectives

An asset-based perspective recognizes that even though caregivers may not support schooling in traditional ways, they have *funds of knowledge* (Moll, Amanti, Neff, & Gonzalez, 1992) such as business knowledge, experience with other countries and cultures, and home and community literacies including those used in church (Lazar, Edwards, & McMillon, 2012). Caregivers also bring *community cultural wealth*, which may include multilingualism, strong family ties, and the ability to navigate various social institutions and community resources (Yosso, 2005).

Additionally, caregivers may have what Yosso (2005) terms *aspirational capital* or "the ability to maintain hopes and dreams for the future, even in the face of real and perceived barriers" (p. 79). Caregivers often provide moral support for their children by stressing the importance of hard work and the value of education (Auerbach, 2007; López, 2001). This reinforcement helps motivate students to succeed.

In the adoption of an asset-based perspective, teachers and administrators develop and/or reaffirm their respect for and understanding of diverse caregivers and their cultures and backgrounds. Often, minority caregivers feel their concerns go unheard by schools (Good, Masewicz, & Vogel, 2010; Lareau & Horvat, 1999). Multilingual Latino caregivers reportedly believe "schools must embrace and respect the culture of the families they serve" (Good et al., 2010, p. 336).

Developing respect and understanding for different cultures is not just about students sharing cultural foods or celebrating a multitude of holidays. Instead, teachers must get to know their students and caregivers as people and individuals, in addition to their cultures, through conversations (Delgado, Huerta, & Campos, 2012). They must bring students' funds of knowledge, experiences, and home literacies into the curriculum and classroom. When children and caregivers see themselves represented in the everyday activities of the class, caregivers begin to believe that the door is open for increased school access and participation.

As a suburban elementary teacher, Lisa observed greater participation from a variety of diverse families at school carnivals and special performances that included their children than at impersonal writing nights that provided the opportunity to meet a famous author. It seems that when students felt invested, either from interest or to showcase their skills, their enthusiasm encouraged the entire family to attend.

Communication

While educators want caregivers' support in helping their children to succeed in school, caregivers cannot help if they are not informed of the needs or requirements. Caregivers frequently feel frustrated when not informed in a timely manner, if at all, about issues regarding their children's grades, behavior, or basic needs, especially before they become problematic (Lareau & Horvat, 1999).

While communication with caregivers should balance successes and struggles, it should also be honest, timely, and understandable. This means that teachers should reach out to caregivers individually about their children when the need arises. It also means that teachers should provide general information that clearly explains what is happening in the classroom (perhaps through newsletters) and describes potential ways caregivers can help their children at home. Clear communication is informative, concise, and avoids the use of educational jargon.

General information can be made accessible to caregivers through paper copies, e-mails, Twitter, blogs, phone messages, Facebook, websites, and the like. However, schools should also be creative in how they reach caregivers such as through meetings over tea/coffee, caregiver phone trees based on language groups, and workshops or buddy systems in which caregivers share information with other caregivers. Schools need to use diverse communication methods to ensure that no caregiver misses information due to lack of access to technology or the inability to read or write.

Additionally, information needs to be in languages that caregivers understand. One day, Lisa called a student's home about tutoring possibilities, and her student's aunt answered. The family spoke Spanish, as did Lisa. Before passing the phone to the student's mother, the aunt asked Lisa about a classroom party in her daughter's class in another grade. She wanted to contribute, but did not know what to do since the communication from her daughter's teacher was in English, not Spanish. Lisa became a link between the family and the school. This experience underscores how caregivers want to participate in their child's education, and can do so if information is provided in understandable ways.

Given the many languages that students' caregivers speak, it is impossible for teachers to be fluent in all of them. However, accommodating caregivers' linguistic needs is critical. To do so, schools can look to the community, other caregivers, and other staff members to help with translating and interpreting. Tools such as Google Translate can be an important first step in communicating with a multilingual community.

Additional resources can be found at New York State Education Department bilingual glossaries (http://www.p12.nysed.gov/biling/bilinged/bilingual_glossaries.htm) and New York University's bilingual glossaries (http://steinhardt.nyu.edu/metrocenter/center/technical_assistance/program/language_rbern/resources/glossary). Both websites offer content-area glossaries for primary and secondary grades in many languages, including Arabic, Bengali, Chinese, Haitian, Hindi, Punjabi, Russian, Spanish, Urdu, and Vietnamese.

Communicating with caregivers in their native languages helps turn one-way communication into two-way communication and understanding. The role of caregivers in schools is not solely to complete the activities with their children that schools ask of them. Caregivers can share valuable information about their children, as they know their children's preferences for learning and solving problems, their strengths and weaknesses, and their motivation and interests (Delgado et al., 2012). Caregivers are invaluable resources, for who really knows their children better?

Schools should foster two-way communication with caregivers. Two-way communication validates children's home lives and learning inside and outside the classroom. It also informs caregivers about what is expected at school while informing teachers about what happens at home. Not only must schools open the door for caregivers through *parentally appropriate* communication, but both parties must also travel back and forth through that door in order to work together to educate children.

Structural Considerations

In order for caregivers to walk through the open door, schools must try to eliminate other roadblocks to school access besides the language of communication. Some roadblocks include caregiver work schedules, childcare needs, transportation issues, and inconvenient or uncomfortable meeting locations. School staff members must facilitate access by knowing caregivers' preferred meeting times and ways of communication. They can offer childcare for meetings by using groups such as Boy/Girl Scouts, community organizations, or secondary school clubs. Moreover, they need to consider the meeting venue. Perhaps caregivers would feel more open and comfortable meeting at a community center rather than the school.

It is not enough to ensure that information about class activities and school initiatives are shared in languages caregivers understand and, at times, places that are convenient for them. Schools must teach caregivers how to navigate the school system and prepare their children for college and/or careers. Schools consciously or unconsciously exclude students and caregivers with the activities they launch because such activities require specific culturally based knowledge and behaviors about the school as an institution (Delgado-Gaitan, 1991).

Often, caregivers who are not middle class, especially not White middle class, do not know the unspoken norms of American schooling, such as how teachers want caregivers to approach them with concerns about their children (Lareau & Horvat, 1999) or the types of classes and service colleges expect (Auerbach, 2004; Suárez-Orozco, Suárez-Orozco, & Todorova, 2008). Caregivers may lack the cultural knowledge and experiences that U.S. education privileges, and they may also lack experience with the U.S. education system. Moreover, they may lack social networks with this knowledge (Gándara & Contreras, 2009; Suárez-Orozco et al., 2008).

Schools should demystify the education process and ensure that all caregivers are on equal footing with knowledge such as expectations for kindergarten, what the grades on report cards measure and mean, and how to prepare students for college and/or careers. If caregivers lack a meaningful context for the information they receive about college and/or career preparation, they need information presented repeatedly in a variety of formats (Auerbach, 2004).

Not only is it important to present information about getting into college, for example, but also information about staying in college is needed (Auerbach, 2004). Caregivers benefit from information about finances, college daily life, and course selection. Latino caregivers respond well to personal testimonies and discussions with other Latino college students. They appreciate the frequent progress updates from their children's teachers and opportunities to meet individually with school faculty and college representatives as well as the support of working through this process with other caregivers in a group (Auerbach, 2004).

Auerbach (2004) recommends that discussions about college planning in caregivers' languages should begin no later than upper elementary school so that caregivers have time to select the necessary classes and prepare their children. Schools should acknowledge the barriers and obstacles students face, and provide strategies for overcoming them. By providing caregivers opportunities to work through the college preparation process with others, caregivers can further develop relationships with the school and other caregivers who have a common background and are facing the same decisions.

However, meetings with families are not successful if their focus is driven solely by the school. Auerbach (2009) found that the most successful programs were not run by district mandates, but instead listened to caregivers' needs and desires, met their literacy levels, and recognized their assets. Successful programs reflected the idea of *differentiated parenting*.

In a study of a project that educated caregivers to teach phonics skills from the district-mandated reading program, Auerbach and Collier (2012) noted little improvement in students' scores. They found that the project "privileged the school agenda and positioned families as deficient in time, interest, or skills to help their children" (p. 28). While educators thought they were educating families about how children could improve their test scores, educators missed an opportunity to listen to caregivers' needs.

Caregivers in Auerbach and Collier's (2012) study wanted to learn ways to motivate their children to read, do homework, or improve their comprehension. Ironically, increased motivation to read improves comprehension (e.g., Guthrie & Klauda, 2014), and increasing motivation would be easier for parents to accomplish than asking them to teach specific phonics skills. Educators missed the important idea that demystifying school processes still involves an asset-based perspective and two-way communication.

CONCLUSION

Caregiver engagement involves a focus on (1) teacher beliefs and mindsets, (2) relationships and communication, and (3) investing families in student goals and helping families monitor student progress and support their learning (Spielberg, 2011). Teachers need to adopt asset-based perspectives that recognize and embrace families' funds of knowledge and community cultural wealth. This is accomplished by completing a demographic profile of the community the school serves, holding conversations with caregivers to learn about their needs, and assessing the degree to which the school meets these needs and welcomes students and their caregivers.

To build relationships and foster communication, schools must accommodate the multiple languages caregivers speak. They must establish two-way communication with caregivers that is honest, concise, meaningful, and frequent. They must share information in ways and at times that fit each caregiver's needs.

Finally, helping caregivers invest in and support students' learning requires that educators demystify the process of schooling. Caregivers must learn early the information, opportunities, and resources their children will need to succeed in the U.S. educational system. This information needs to be repeated in multiple formats with opportunities to work through it individually and collaboratively. As schools respond to caregivers' needs and desires for information, they must understand that top-down mandates do not seem to lead to increased achievement for *all* students. Only through collaborative efforts where all claim ownership is change possible.

REFLECTION QUESTIONS

1. If you feel that caregivers at your school are disengaged, what might be some underlying reasons?
2. How can your school begin building trust and understanding with the community it serves?

3. In what ways does your school create involvement opportunities based on caregivers' expectations and needs? How are current involvement opportunities increasing or not increasing student achievement?

REFERENCES

Auerbach, S. (2004). Engaging Latino parents in supporting college pathways: Lessons from a college access program. *Journal of Hispanic Higher Education, 3*(2), 125–145.

Auerbach, S. (2007). From moral supporters to struggling advocates: Reconceptualizing parent roles in education through the experience of working-class families of color. *Urban Education, 42*(3), 250–283.

Auerbach, S. (2009). Walking the walk: Portraits in leadership for family engagement in urban schools. *School Community Journal, 19*(1), 9.

Auerbach, S., & Collier, S. (2012). Bringing high stakes from the classroom to the parent center: Lessons from an intervention program for immigrant families. *Teachers College Record, 114*(3), 1–40.

Badger, E. (2014, December 10). Life in the suburbs means something very different for Whites and Blacks. *Washington Post.* Retrieved from https://www.washingtonpost.com/news/wonk/wp/2014/12/10/how-life-in-the-suburbs-means-something-very-different-for-whites-and-blacks

Boutte, G. S., & Johnson, G. (2013). Community and family involvement in urban schools. In H. R. Milner & K. Lomotey (Eds.), *Handbook on urban education* (pp. 167–182). New York, NY: Routledge.

Delgado, R., Huerta, M. E., & Campos, D. (2012). Enhancing relationships with parents of English language learners. *Principal Leadership, 12*(6), 30–34.

Delgado-Gaitan, C. (1991). Involving parents in the schools: A process of empowerment. *American Journal of Education, 100*(1), 20–46.

Drayton, T. (2015). *5 reasons not to move Black kids to White suburbs.* Retrieved from http://www.clutchmagonline.com/2015/09/5-reasons-not-to-move-black-kids-to-suburbs

Edwards, P. A. (2004). *Children's literacy development: Making it happen through school, family, and community involvement.* Boston, MA: Allyn & Bacon.

Edwards, P. A. (2009). *Tapping the potential of parents: A strategic guide to boosting student achievement through family involvement.* New York, NY: Scholastic.

Edwards, P. A. (2016). *New ways to engage parents: Strategies and tools for teachers and leaders, K–12.* New York, NY: Teachers College Press.

Fields-Smith, C. (2005). African American parents before and after *Brown. Journal of Curriculum and Supervision, 29*(2), 129–135.

Gándara, P. C., & Contreras, F. (2009). *The Latino education crisis: The consequences of failed social policies.* Cambridge, MA: Harvard University Press.

Gill, S., Posamentier, J., & Hill, P. T. (2016). *Suburban schools: The unrecognized frontier in public education.* Retrieved from: http://www.crpe.org/publications/suburban-schools-unrecognized-frontier-public-education

Goldenberg, C. (2001). Making schools work for low-income families in the 21st century. In S. B. Neuman & D. K. Dickinson (Eds.), *Handbook of early literacy research* (pp. 211–231). New York, NY: The Guilford Press.

Good, M. E., Masewicz, S., & Vogel, L. (2010). Latino English language learners: Bridging achievement and cultural gaps between schools and families. *Journal of Latinos and Education, 9*(4), 321–339.

Guthrie, J. T., & Klauda, S. L. (2014). Effects of classroom practices on reading comprehension, engagement, and motivations for adolescents. *Reading Research Quarterly, 49*(4), 387–416.

Henderson, A. T., & Mapp, K. L. (2002). A new wave of evidence: The impact of school, family, and community connections on student achievement. Austin, TX: Southwest Educational Development Laboratory.

Howard, G. R. (2007). As diversity grows, so must we. *Educational Leadership, 64*(6), 16–22.

Iowa Parent Information Resource Center. (2008). *Parent-friendly schools—Starting the conversation: 5 tools for schools*. Retrieved from http://www.heartlandaea.org/media/documents/Parent_Friendly_Schools_E52DE9605B233.pdf

Johnson, L. (2015). Rethinking parental involvement: A critical review of the literature. *Urban Education Research and Policy Annuals, 3*(1). Retrieved from https://journals.uncc.edu/urbaned/article/view/354/349.

Kneebone, E., & Berube, A. (2013). *Confronting suburban poverty in America*. Washington, DC: Brookings Institution Press.

Lareau, A., & Horvat, E. M. (1999). Moments of social inclusion and exclusion race, class, and cultural capital in family-school relationships. *Sociology of Education, 72*(1), 37–53.

Lazar, A. M., Edwards, P. A., & McMillon, G. T. (2012). *Bridging literacy and equity: The essential guide to social equity teaching*. New York, NY: Teachers College Press.

López, G. R. (2001). The value of hard work: Lessons on parent involvement from an (im)migrant household. *Harvard Educational Review, 71*(3), 416–438.

López, G. R., Scribner, J. D., & Mahitivanichcha, K. (2001). Redefining parental involvement: Lessons from high-performing migrant-impacted schools. *American Educational Research Journal, 38*(2), 253–288.

Milner IV, H. R. (2015). *Rac(e)ing to class: Confronting poverty and race in schools and classrooms*. Cambridge, MA: Harvard Education Press.

Moll, L. C., Amanti, C., Neff, D., & Gonzalez, N. (1992). Funds of knowledge for teaching: Using a qualitative approach to connect homes and classrooms. *Theory into Practice, 31*(2), 132–141.

Noguera, P. (2001). The role and influence of environmental and cultural factors on the cultural factors on the academic performance of African American males. *Urban Education, 38*(4), 431–459.

Prater, D. L., Bermudez, A. B., & Owens, E. (1997). Examining parental involvement in rural, urban, and suburban schools. *Journal of Research in Rural Education, 13*(1), 72–75.

Robinson, K., & Harris, A. L. (2014, April 12). Parental involvement is overrated. *New York Times*. Retrieved from http://opinionator.blogs.nytimes.com/2014/04/12/parental-involvement-is-overrated/?_r=1

Spielberg, L. (2011). *Successful family engagement in the classroom: What teachers need to know and be able to do to engage families in raising student achievement?* Cambridge, MA: Harvard Family Research Project & Flamboyan Foundation. Retrieved from http://eric.ed.gov/?id=ED517975

Suárez-Orozco, C., Suárez-Orozco, M. M., & Todorova, I. (2008). *Learning a new land: Immigrant students in American society*. Cambridge, MA: Harvard University Press.

Underhill, J. (n.d.). Is your school parent-friendly? *PTO Today*. Retrieved from https://www.ptotoday.com/pto-today-articles/article/398-is-your-school-parent-friendly

Whitehurst, G. J., & Longigan, C. J. (2002). Emergent literacy: Development from prereaders to readers. In S. B. Neuman & D. K. Dickinson (Eds.), *Handbook of early literacy research* (pp. 11–29). New York, NY: The Guilford Press.

Yan, W. (2000). Preparing students for the new millennium: Exploring factors that contribute to the successful education of African American students. *Journal of Negro Education, 68*(1), 5–22.

Yosso, T. J. (2005). Whose culture has capital? A critical race theory discussion of community cultural wealth. *Race, Ethnicity and Education, 8*(1), 69–91.

About the Authors

Carl L. Bankston III is professor of sociology at Tulane University, where he teaches sociology of education, international migration, research methods, and social stratification. His most recent books include *The Rise of the New Second Generation, Controls and Choices: The Educational Marketplace and the Failure of School Desegregation, Still Failing: The Continuing Failure of School Desegregation*, and *Immigrant Networks and Social Capital*. Carl has published a number of other books as author or editor, as well as over one hundred journal articles and book chapters. His primary research areas are sociology of education and international migration.

Stephen J. Caldas is professor of educational leadership at Manhattanville College, Purchase, New York, where he teaches doctoral students educational policy and the suite of statistics courses. His recent books are *Still Failing: The Continuing Paradox of School Desegregation* and *Controls and Choices: The Educational Marketplace and the Failure of School Desegregation*. Stephen has authored or coauthored more than seventy-five articles and book chapters. His research interests center around the social, policy, and legal contexts of education, with specific expertise in the use of advanced multivariate statistics.

Lisa Domke was an elementary teacher for eight years in a suburban school district in western Michigan. She worked with many language learners both in general education and Spanish immersion. She worked in a Michigan summer migrant education program, and taught literacy courses at Michigan State University and Grand Valley State University. Lisa is pursuing a Ph.D. at Michigan State University specializing in literacy, language learning, and emergent bilinguals/English learners. Her research focuses on biliteracy—how children develop literacy skills in multiple languages.

Patricia A. Edwards, a member of the Reading Hall of Fame, is a professor of language and literacy at Michigan State University. She served on the International Reading Association (IRA) Board of Directors, as the first African American president of the Literacy Research Association, and president of the IRA. She has published numerous articles, two family literacy programs, and seven books, including *A Path to Follow: Learning to Listen to Parents*, *Tapping the Potential of Parents: A Strategic Guide to Boosting Student Achievement Through Family Involvement*, and *New Ways to Engage Parents: Strategies and Tools for Teachers and Leaders, K–12.*

Douglas Fisher is professor of educational leadership at San Diego State University and a teacher leader at Health Sciences High. He is the recipient of an IRA Celebrate Literacy award, the Farmer award for excellence in writing from NCTE, and a Christa McAuliffe award for excellence in teacher education. He has published numerous articles on reading and literacy, differentiated instruction, and curriculum design as well as books, such as *Text Complexity: Raising Rigor in Reading*, *Common Core English Language Arts in a PLC at Work*, *Rigorous Reading*, and *The School Leader's Guide to Teaching English Learners.*

Erica Frankenberg is associate professor of education and demography at Pennsylvania State University, and codirector of the Center for Education and Civil Rights. Her research interests focus on racial desegregation and inequality in K–12 schools, school choice and segregation, and the connections between school segregation and other metropolitan policies particularly in suburban communities. She has published more than fifty peer-reviewed articles. Her recently published books include *The Resegregation of Suburban Schools: A Hidden Crisis in American Education* and *Integrating Schools in a Changing Society: New Policies and Legal Options for a Multiracial Generation.*

Nancy Frey is professor of educational leadership at San Diego State University and the recipient of the 2008 Early Career Achievement Award from the National Reading Conference. Nancy has published in *The Reading Teacher*, *Journal of Adolescent and Adult Literacy*, *English Journal*, *Voices in the Middle*, *Middle School Journal*, and *Educational Leadership*. She and Douglas Fisher have coauthored several books on literacy development, including *Visible Learning for Literacy*. Nancy is a credentialed special educator, reading specialist, and administrator in California, and teaches at Health Sciences High and Middle College.

Eugene García is professor emeritus at Arizona State University. He served as professor, vice president for education partnerships, and dean of the Mary Lou Fulton College of Education at ASU. He was a senior officer in the U.S. Department of Education. He received an honorary doctorate from the Erikson Institute, and is an AERA fellow. He has published extensively in early learning, bilingual development, and equal educational opportunity. His recent books include *Bilingualism and Cognition: Informing Bilingual Research, Pedagogy and Policy* and *Understanding the Language Development and Early Education of Hispanic Children.*

María Paula Ghiso is assistant professor at Teachers College, Columbia University. Her research investigates literacy in multilingual and transnational contexts. María Paula is a former New York City dual language teacher and has facilitated professional development on language and literacy learning in a range of contexts. She has published in venues such as *Journal of Early Childhood Literacy, Teachers College Record, Research in the Teaching of English, Language Arts, Harvard Educational Review,* and *Journal of Literacy Research.* She is a coauthor of the book *Partnering with Immigrant Communities: Action through Literacy.*

Diane W. Gómez is associate professor of second languages and chairperson for the Department of Educational Leadership and Special Subjects at Manhattanville College. Her research interests include multicultural and multilingual education, literacy in the context of dual language, and second language programs. She has coauthored several articles and book chapters related to multilingual learners and professional development. She has coauthored two books, *Literacy Leadership in Changing Schools: Ten Keys for Successful Professional Development* and *Changing Suburbs, Changing Students: Helping School Leaders Face the Challenges.*

Stephen Kotok is assistant professor of educational leadership and foundations at the University of Texas at El Paso. He formerly taught middle school social studies in Philadelphia and served as the middle school leader in Asbury Park, New Jersey. His research focuses on the extent that school climate, organization, school choice, and segregation influence student learning and attainment. His recent work has appeared in the *American Journal of Education, Educational Policy,* and the *Peabody Journal of Education.* He has also produced policy reports for the Civil Rights Project/Proyecto Derechos Civiles at UCLA and the Center for Rural Pennsylvania.

Shelley B. Wepner is dean and professor of education in the School of Education of Manhattanville College. Her research focuses on connections between K–12 education and higher education and leadership skills for effectively supporting teacher education and literacy development. She has published over 145 articles, book chapters, award-winning software packages, and books. Her most recently published books are *Literacy Leadership in Changing Schools: Ten Keys for Successful Professional Development, Changing Suburbs, Changing Students: Helping School Leaders Face the Challenges*, and *The Administration and Supervision of Reading Programs*, fifth edition.

Kristen White was a primary classroom teacher, a K–5 school media specialist and technology teacher, and a middle school Spanish teacher for over ten years. Kristen provided professional development to teachers, administrators, and parents on the Orton-Gillingham reading methodology with the Institute for Multisensory Education. She taught literacy courses at Michigan State University. Kristen is pursuing a Ph.D. at Michigan State University in curriculum, instruction, and teacher education with a literacy specialization. Her research focuses on how prospective teachers learn to teach literacy.

Debbie Zacarian is the founder of Zacarian & Associates and the Center for English Language Education and Advancing Student Achievement at the Collaborative for Educational Services, Northampton, Massachusetts. She previously taught at the University of Massachusetts–Amherst, and directed the Amherst Public Schools' English learner and bilingual programs. Her professional books include *In It Together: How Student, Family and Community Partnerships Advance Engagement and Achievement in Diverse Classrooms, Mastering Academic Language: A Framework for Supporting Student Achievement, The Essential Guide for Educating Beginning English Learners*, and *Transforming Schools for English Learners: A Comprehensive Framework for School Leaders*.

www.ingramcontent.com/pod-product-compliance
Lightning Source LLC
Chambersburg PA
CBHW020356270326
41926CB00007B/457